EQUALITY *and*
EFFICIENCY

THE BROOKINGS CLASSICS

Thoughtful, relevant, and timely books have been the hallmark of the Brookings Institution Press since its founding, and the press has been fortunate to count among its authors some of the most important thinkers of the twentieth century. With The Brookings Classics the press draws on its vast library of original work to reintroduce some of its most influential books to new audiences. Each book in the series has made important contributions to policy debates and scholarly discourse and has stood the test of time to remain relevant in today's world. Each Classic also includes a foreword written by an influential thinker in his or her field, explaining the book's significance while grounding the work in a contemporary context.

Check out the Brookings website to learn more about the individual titles in the series: www.brookings/edu/classics.

The Irony of Vietnam: The System Worked
Leslie Gelb with Richard K. Betts

Development Projects Observed
Albert O. Hirschman

Red Tape: Its Origins, Uses, and Abuses
Herbert Kaufman

Equality and Efficiency: The Big Tradeoff
Arthur M. Okun

Camp David: Peacemaking and Politics
William B. Quandt

Systematic Thinking for Social Action
Alice M. Rivlin

ARTHUR M. OKUN

EQUALITY *and* EFFICIENCY

The Big Tradeoff

FOREWORD BY LAWRENCE SUMMERS

BROOKINGS INSTITUTION PRESS
Washington, D.C.

This book is a revised and expanded version of material originally
delivered in April 1974 as a Godkin Lecture at the John F. Kennedy School
of Government, Harvard University. The Godkin Lectures on the Essentials
of Free Government and the Duties of the Citizen were established at Harvard
University in 1903 in memory of Edwin Lawrence Godkin (1831–1902).

The final chapter, "Further Thoughts on Equality and Efficiency," is reprinted from
Colin D. Campbell, ed., *Income Redistribution* (American Enterprise Institute for
Public Policy Research, 1977), and used with permission.

The first Brookings edition of *Equality and Efficiency* was published in 1975.

The Brookings Institution is a private nonprofit organization devoted to research,
education, and publication on important issues of domestic and foreign policy. Its
principal purpose is to bring the highest-quality independent research and analysis
to bear on current and emerging policy problems. Interpretations or conclusions in
Brookings publications should be understood to be solely those of the authors.

Library of Congress Cataloging-in-Publication data

Okun, Arthur M.
  Equality and efficiency : the big tradeoff / Arthur M. Okun ; foreword by
Lawrence Summers.
    pages cm — (The Brookings Classics)
  "This book is a revised and expanded version of material originally
delivered in April 1974 as a Godkin Lecture at the John F. Kennedy School
of Government, Harvard University."
  Includes bibliographical references and index.
  ISBN 978-0-8157-2653-1 (pbk. : alk. paper) — ISBN 978-0-8157-2654-8 (e-book)
  1. Comparative economics. 2. Equality. I. Title.

  HB90.O38 2015
  330—dc23   2015006126

Printed on acid-free paper

Typeset in Sabon

Composition by Cynthia Stock
Silver Spring, Maryland

CONTENTS

FOREWORD

I still remember the excitement with which I first read Arthur Okun's *Equality and Efficiency: The Big Tradeoff* as a first-year graduate student. It was the antithesis of the first-year economic theory sequence in which I was mired: a thoughtful, engaging, rigorously logical analysis of real issues that were crucial to the well-being of the American people. His text helped me realize that I had become an economist because I, like Okun, wanted to devote my career to thinking about—and on occasion to helping to act on—major public policy issues.

I was impressed and influenced especially by two aspects of Okun's analysis. First, he emphasized the good reasons why many things, even in capitalist economies, are not for sale—a very useful antidote to my youthful infatuation with the notion that mutual voluntary exchange was presumptively beneficial. Second, Okun's leaky bucket experiment provided a compelling way to think about the tradeoffs involved in using taxes and transfers to redistribute income. I remember burdening my friends for weeks with questions about whether it would be good to take $100 from someone with an income of $200,000 and give $50 to someone with an income of $50,000.

Rereading *Equality and Efficiency: The Big Tradeoff* after forty years, I am struck at one level by how well it reads and at another by how much the world has changed. On what one might think of as questions of "economic philosophy," I doubt that Okun has been improved on in the subsequent interval. His discussion of how societies rely on rights as well as markets should be required reading for all young economists who are enamored with market solutions to all problems. He is careful and rigorous in drawing out Polanyi's insights regarding the broader social systems in which markets must reside.[1] Indeed, Okun largely anticipates the main tenets of Michael Sandel's recent critique of markets when he discusses what would be wrong with permitting individuals to pay a fee to hire a substitute for jury duty or authorizing those conscripted to buy their way out of military service or allowing people to sell themselves into some form of bondage.[2]

Okun's development of the theme that "the market has its place, but must be kept in its place" was prescient with respect to the governing philosophy adopted by the Clinton administration in the United States during the 1990s and by "New Labor" in the United Kingdom around that same period. Okun rightly emphasizes the dangers of excessive interference with markets while simultaneously stressing that markets without public action are unlikely to produce distributional outcomes that are sustainable in a democracy. His emphasis on access to education on an equal basis for all and on the need for taxes and transfers in many ways anticipated the Clinton administration's focus on "Putting People First."[3]

However, much has happened in the last four decades that Okun did not and probably could not have anticipated.

— Okun wrote that productivity growth had supported steady increases in median family incomes and reductions in poverty for more than a generation. Yet, since the mid-1970s, productivity

1. Karl Polanyi, "Our Obsolete Market Mentality," in George Dalton, ed., *Primitive, Archaic, and Modern Economies* (Beacon, 1971), pp. 59–77.

2. Michael J. Sandel, "What Money Can't Buy: The Moral Limits of Markets" (Macmillan, 2012).

3. This was a Clinton campaign slogan as well as a policy memorandum released during the campaign. Governor Bill Clinton and Senator Al Gore, "Putting People First: How We All Change America" (Times Books, September 1992).

growth has slowed and growth in median family income has been minimal.

—Okun noted that the U.S. income distribution had been relatively stable over the post–World War II period. But, a few years following *Equality and Efficiency*'s publication, the distribution of income started to become steadily more unequal, with the share of income going to the top 1 percent rising from about 8 percent at the end of the 1970s to about 20 percent today.[4]

—Okun took essentially no account of the openness of the U.S. economy in discussing efficiency and equity. Today, concerns that global economic integration is hurting workers—especially the unskilled—frames debates about trade policy and much else. In particular, commerce with countries where wage rates were less than one-fifth of U.S. levels was a minor economic phenomenon in the 1970s, but it is a major one today. In 1979, total U.S.-China trade was $2 billion; in 2013, it totaled $562 billion.[5]

—Okun focuses on the problems of poverty and of the middle class. The outsized gains enjoyed by a very small minority of the population have emerged today as a major economic issue. In 1965, the ratio of CEO compensation to the compensation of the average worker was about 20:1. Today it is 331:1.[6] In the same period, the financial sector, which paid average wages at the time Okun wrote, has emerged as a major source of great fortunes.

—When Okun wrote *Equality and Efficiency*, the American economy was much less fluid than it is today. It was unheard of for start-up companies to become major forces in the economy within a few years the way that Google, Facebook, and Amazon have

4. French economist Thomas Piketty has written extensively about this rise. See, for example, Thomas Piketty, *Capital in the Twenty-First Century* (Belknap Press, 2014).

5. Wayne M. Morrison, "China-U.S. Trade Issues" (Congressional Research Service, December 2014).

6. Lawrence Mishel and Alyssa Davis, "CEO Pay Continues to Rise as Typical Workers Are Paid Less" (Economic Policy Institute, June 2014); AFL-CIO Executive Paywatch 2014.

done. Many fewer workers worked on their own as independent contractors. Firms were much more tied to their communities and relied much less on complex supply chains.

Tragically, Arthur Okun died in 1980 at the age of 51, so he did not see these developments. Had he lived, I have no doubt that America would have addressed them all more wisely. He was always aware that economists confront a constantly changing reality and that their theories and policy recommendations can never stand still. Thus, he would have been prepared to amend his views in the face of new evidence and to propose novel solutions to emergent problems.

As a way of thinking about where analysis and policy should go, I found it helpful to ask myself what Okun would say about the major economic changes just described if he were revising *Equality and Efficiency* today. Here are my best guesses:

First, Okun would recognize that stagnation in middle-class incomes is a central issue for democracies. He would empha- size the importance of a constructive supply-side agenda that embraces the development of human capital, scientific knowl- edge, public infrastructure, and business investment. It would have been very much in character for him to warn egalitarians that redistribution of a rapidly growing pie would be much easier than redistribution of a pie that was not growing. He also would warn that the level and growth of GDP were far from sufficient statistics for gauging economic success, as issues of distribution of income are central.

Second, Okun would have been very disturbed by the rapid growth in incomes at the top of the distribution. I am quite confi- dent that if he were writing today he would have been even more emphatic in urging reform to make taxes more progressive. And he would have skewered suggestions that tax burdens were inhib- iting investment at a time like the present when costs of capital are at near record low levels. At the same time, I expect he would have counseled against a "politics of envy" and reminded his readers that the possibility of making a great fortune can be a powerful spur to innovation and entrepreneurship.

Third, Okun would, I suspect, have had great sympathy for those who pointed out the adverse impacts of globalization on disadvantaged workers. He would have empathized with complaints that outsourcing leads to the hollowing out of traditional industrial sectors. But, in line with his generally balanced approach, I suspect that he would nonetheless have supported well-designed policy packages that promoted trade. He would insist that trade could produce a bigger pie but that ways must be found to ensure that all share in its benefits.

Fourth, Okun would have been both surprised and appalled that deflation had become as much an American economic challenge as inflation. And he would have been very troubled by the retreat from work by middle-aged men. The idea that even when the economy is near full employment, more than one in seven men between the ages of 25 and 54 are not working would have left him profoundly dissatisfied. In all likelihood, with inflation quiescent, he would have been more emphatic about the benefits of a high-pressure economy than when he was writing in 1975.[7] He would have insisted on the use of both fiscal and monetary policy to employ as many people as possible.

Fifth, Okun would, I imagine, have engaged in some way with the widespread loss of confidence in government and other institutions that has become manifest over the last long generation. I am not sure what he would have concluded. I imagine he would have been troubled by our current approach to balancing the goals

7. Okun drew on the work of Henry C. Wallich when he characterized macroeconomists as advocates of "high-pressure" and "low-pressure" operations of the economy. High-pressure proponents argued for fuller utilization of labor and capital despite the possibility of increased inflation, while low-pressure advocates were more concerned about the potential costs of increased inflation. See Henry C. Wallich, "Conservative Economic Policy," *Yale Review*, Vol. 46 (Autumn 1956); Arthur M. Okun, "Upward Mobility in a High-Pressure Economy," *Brookings Papers on Economic Activity*, Vol. 4, no. 1 (1973).

of free speech on the one hand and limiting the role of money in politics on the other. I suspect he would have been sympathetic to the objective of improving government performance to restore the faith of citizens. He would have struggled with issues related to health care, where he would have seen so much market imperfection, but so much public imperfection as well.

We will never know all that Okun could have taught us. But it is a tribute to his humane wisdom and deep seriousness of purpose that this book, while topical four decades ago, repays study today. I hope and expect that this new edition of *Equality and Efficiency: The Big Tradeoff* will inspire young economists as much as it inspired me forty years ago.

LAWRENCE H. SUMMERS

Cambridge, Mass.
January 2015

CHAPTER ONE

RIGHTS AND DOLLARS

American society proclaims the worth of every human being. All citizens are guaranteed equal justice and equal political rights. Everyone has a pledge of speedy response from the fire department and access to national monuments. As American citizens, we are all members of the same club.

Yet at the same time, our institutions say "find a job or go hungry," "succeed or suffer." They prod us to get ahead of our neighbors economically after telling us to stay in line socially. They award prizes that allow the big winners to feed their pets better than the losers can feed their children.

Such is the double standard of a capitalist democracy, professing and pursuing an egalitarian political and social system and simultaneously generating gaping disparities in economic well-being. This mixture of equality and inequality sometimes smacks of inconsistency and even insincerity. Yet I believe that, in many cases, the institutional arrangements represent uneasy compromises rather than fundamental inconsistencies. The contrasts among American families in living standards and in material wealth reflect a system of rewards and penalties that is intended to encourage effort and channel it into socially productive activity. To the extent that the system succeeds, it generates an efficient economy. But that pursuit of efficiency necessarily creates inequalities. And hence society faces a tradeoff between equality and efficiency.

Tradeoffs are the central study of the economist. "You can't have your cake and eat it too" is a good candidate for the fundamental theorem of economic analysis. Producing more of one thing means using labor and capital that could be devoted to more output of something else. Consuming more now means saving less for the future. Working longer impinges on leisure. The crusade against inflation demands the sacrifice of output and employment—posing the tradeoff that now concerns the nation most seriously.

I have specialized throughout my career on the tradeoff between inflation and unemployment. To put it mildly, the search for a satisfactory way of managing it has not yet been successfully completed. I, for one, have not given up; indeed, I plan to spend the rest of my professional life on that problem. But in this essay I am wandering away from my usual concerns briefly to discuss an even more nagging and pervasive tradeoff, that between equality and efficiency. It is, in my view, our biggest socioeconomic tradeoff, and it plagues us in dozens of dimensions of social policy. We can't have our cake of market efficiency and share it equally.

To the economist, as to the engineer, efficiency means getting the most out of a given input. The inputs applied in production are human effort, the services of physical capital such as machines and buildings, and the endowments of nature like land and mineral resources. The outputs are thousands of different types of goods and services. If society finds a way, with the same inputs, to turn out more of some products (and no less of the others), it has scored an increase in efficiency.

This concept of efficiency implies that more is better, insofar as the "more" consists of items that people want to buy. In relying on the verdicts of consumers as indications of what they want, I, like other economists, accept people's choices as reasonably rational expressions of what makes them better off. To be sure, by a different set of criteria, it is appropriate to ask skeptically whether people are made better off (and thus whether society really becomes more efficient) through the production of more whiskey, more cigarettes, and more big cars. That inquiry raises several intriguing further questions. Why do people want the things they buy? How are their choices influenced by education, advertising, and the like? Are there criteria by which welfare can be appraised that are superior to the observation of the choices people make? Without defense and without apology, let me simply state that I will not explore those issues despite their importance. That merely reflects my choices, and I hope they are accepted as reasonably rational.

I have greater conviction in essentially ignoring a second type of criticism of the "more is better" concept of efficiency. Some warn that the economic growth that generates more output today may plunder the earth of its resources and make for lower standards of living in the future. Other economists have recently accepted the challenge of the "doomsday" school and, in my judgment, have effectively refuted its dire predictions.[1]

The concept of economic equality also poses its problems, which I shall explore more fully in chapter 3. Impressionistically, I shall speak of more or less equality as implying smaller or greater disparities among families in their maintainable standards of living, which in turn implies lesser or greater disparities in the distribution of income and wealth, relative to the needs of families of different sizes. Equal standards of living would not mean that people would choose to spend their incomes and allocate their wealth identically. Economic equality would not mean sameness or drabness or uniformity, because people have vastly different tastes and preferences. Within any income stratum today, some families spend far more on housing and far less on education than do others. Economic equality is obviously different from equality

---

1. See William D. Nordhaus, "World Dynamics: Measurement without Data," *Economic Journal,* Vol. 83 (December 1973), pp. 1156–83; and Robert M. Solow, "Is the End of the World at Hand?" in Andrew Weintraub, Eli Schwartz, and J. Richard Aronson (eds.), *The Economic Growth Controversy* (International Arts and Sciences Press, 1973), pp. 39–61.

of opportunity, as I shall use the terms, and I shall explore that distinction further in chapter 3.

The presence of a tradeoff between efficiency and equality does not mean that everything that is good for one is necessarily bad for the other. Measures that might soak the rich so much as to destroy investment and hence impair the quality and quantity of jobs for the poor could worsen both efficiency and equality. On the other hand, techniques that improve the productivity and earnings potential of unskilled workers might benefit society with greater efficiency *and* greater equality. Nonetheless, there are places where the two goals conflict, and those pose the problems. The conflicts in the economic sphere will be discussed in chapter 2, which will analyze the ways that the market creates inequality and efficiency jointly, and in chapter 4, which will examine the ways that federal policy attempts to nudge the distribution of wealth and income generated by the market toward greater equality by such measures as progressive taxation, social insurance, welfare, and jobs programs.

In this chapter, I will examine the ways in which American society promotes equality (and pays some costs in terms of efficiency) by establishing social and political rights that are distributed equally and universally and that are intended to be kept out of the marketplace. Those rights affect the functioning of the economy and, at the same time, their operation is affected by the market. They lie basically in the territory of the political scientist, which is rarely invaded by the economist. But at times the economist cannot afford to ignore them. The interrelationships between market institutions and inequality are clarified when set against the background of the entire social structure, including the areas where equality is given high priority.

A society that is both democratic and capitalistic has a split-level institutional structure, and both levels need to be surveyed. When only the capitalistic level is inspected, issues concerning the distribution of material welfare are out of focus. In an economy

that is based primarily on private enterprise, public efforts to promote equality represent a deliberate interference with the results
generated by the marketplace, and they are rarely costless. When
the question is posed as: "Should the government tamper with
the market?" the self-evident answer is a resounding "No." Not
surprisingly, this is a common approach among anti-egalitarian
writers. Forget that the Declaration of Independence proclaims
the equality of human beings, ignore the Bill of Rights, and one
can write that only intellectuals—as distinguished sharply from
people—care much about equality.[2] With these blinders firmly in
place, egalitarianism in economics can be investigated as though it
were an idiosyncrasy, perhaps even a type of neurosis.[3]

It is just as one-sided to view enormous wealth or huge incomes
as symptoms of vicious or evil behavior by their owners, or as an
oversight of an egalitarian society. The institutions of a market
economy promote such inequality, and they are as much a part
of our social framework as the civil and political institutions that
pursue egalitarian goals. To some, "profits" and "rich" may be
dirty words, but their views have not prevailed in the rules of the
economic game.

To get a proper perspective, even an economist with no training in other social sciences had better tread—or at least tiptoe—
into social and political territory. And that is where I shall begin.
I shall travel through the places where society deliberately opts
for equality, noting the ways these choices compromise efficiency
and curb the role of the market, and examining the reasons why
society may choose to distribute some of its entitlements equally.
I shall focus particularly on some of the difficulties in establishing

---

2. Irving Kristol, "About Equality," *Commentary,* Vol. 54 (November 1972),
pp. 41–47.
3. Harry G. Johnson, "Some Micro-Economic Reflections on Income and Wealth
Inequalities," *Annals of the American Academy of Political and Social Science,* Vol.
409 (September 1973), p. 54. Johnson attributes the concern with inequality, in part,
to "a naive and basically infantile anthropomorphism."

and implementing the principle that the equally distributed rights ought not to be bought and sold for money.

THE DOMAIN OF RIGHTS

A vast number of entitlements and privileges are distributed universally and equally and free of charge to all adult citizens of the United States. Our laws bestow upon us the right to obtain equal justice, to exercise freedom of speech and religion, to vote, to take a spouse and procreate, to be free in our persons in the sense of immunity from enslavement, to disassociate ourselves from American society by emigration, as well as various claims on public services such as police protection and public education. For convenience, I shall call all of these universal entitlements "rights," recognizing that this is a broader use of the term than most political theorists employ and that it lumps together freedom of speech and free access to visit the Capitol.

Rights have their negative side as well, in the form of certain duties that are imposed on all citizens. For example, everyone has a responsibility to obey the law—anyone who would merely balance the cost of risking a prison sentence against the benefits obtainable from stealing a wallet is violating that duty. Military conscription and jury service are examples of duties assigned—in principle, if not always in practice—by random selection and not according to the preferences or status of individuals.

Features of Rights

An obvious feature of rights—in sharp contrast with economic assets—is that they are acquired and exercised without any monetary charge. Because citizens do not normally have to pay a price for using their rights,[4] they lack the usual incentive to economize

4. Money may be relevant indirectly. Visiting the Capitol involves the cost of transportation. More seriously, the cost of obtaining equal justice before the law creates problems discussed later in this chapter.

on exercising them. If the fire department charged for its services, people would be at least a little more reluctant to turn in an alarm and perhaps a bit more systematic about fire prevention. If speaking out on public issues had a price tag, citizens might be more thoughtful before they sounded off—and perhaps that would improve the quality of debate. But society does not try to ration the exercise of rights.

Second, because rights are universally distributed, they do not invoke the economist's principle of comparative advantage that tells people to specialize in the things they do particularly well. Everybody can get into the act, including some who are not talented actors. Some people with great skill in their civilian pursuits make hopelessly inept soldiers; thus, the draft cannot provide the most efficient army, yet it is the way we raise wartime military forces. Surely, voters do not have equal ability, equal information or education, or an equal stake in political decisions. Since those decisions are concentrated on taxing and spending, property owners and taxpayers may have a greater stake in them; that relative difference is ignored in the acceptance of universal suffrage. We have dismissed Edmund Burke's contention that a limitation of suffrage to property owners might help to ensure a thoughtful approach to social policy.[5] Similarly, although children are excluded from voting rights, we forgo the use of even a minimum test of competence like literacy as a qualification.

We have rejected John Stuart Mill's proposal that differential voting powers should be based on achievement and intelligence, despite his insistence that such a system was "not . . . necessarily invidious . . ."[6] Recently, a writer on the op-ed page of the *New York Times* reinvented Mill's wheel, proposing a "system of proportional representation that would weight each man's vote

5. Edmund Burke, *Reflections on the Revolution in France* (1st ed., 1790; Penguin Books, 1969), pp. 140–41.
6. John Stuart Mill, *Considerations on Representative Government* (1st ed., 1875; Bobbs-Merrill, 1958), p. 136.

in proportion to his demonstrated capability to make intelligent choices."[7] Such proposals imply that the division of labor is relevant to the distribution of voting rights, and given that fundamental premise, they might make sense. But rejecting that premise, many of us find them preposterous.

A third characteristic of rights is that they are not distributed as incentives, or as rewards and penalties. Unlike the dollar prizes of the marketplace or the nonpecuniary honors and awards elsewhere, extra rights and duties are not used to channel behavior into socially constructive pursuits. In principle, people could be offered extra votes or exemptions from the draft in recognition of outstanding performance, and those rewards might serve as added incentives to productive achievement. But only in a few limited and extreme cases, like the loss of the right to vote by convicted felons, does society establish a quid pro quo in the domain of rights.

A century ago, that advocate of thoroughgoing laissez-faire, Herbert Spencer, opposed a host of universally distributed public services, resting his criticisms on several grounds, including disincentive effects. Even public libraries drew his scorn.[8] After all, they offer people real income without requiring any effort in return. Indeed, free books may be doubly damned because they are a form of real income that increases the value of leisure. Spencer certainly was revealing some bizarre social attitudes, but he had a point in recognizing the inefficiency of rights.[9]

Fourth, the distribution of rights stresses equality even at the expense of equity and freedom. When people differ in capabilities, interests, and preferences, identical treatment is not equitable treatment, at least by some standards. It would be hard to

7. Joseph Farkas, "One Man, 1/4 Vote," *New York Times,* March 29, 1974.
8. Herbert Spencer, *The Man versus the State* (Appleton, 1884), p. 33.
9. To be sure, the efficiency argument is not clear-cut for public libraries, since access to books may build human capital.

defend the provision of public education out of tax revenue as equitable to the childless or the patrons of private schools, however compelling its other merits. People are not forced to exercise their rights—freedom of speech includes the right to be silent, and universal suffrage does not impose a requirement to go to the polls. But duties clearly encroach on freedom. Moreover, people are forcibly prevented from buying and selling rights; and that deprives them of freedom.

That important principle—that rights cannot be bought and sold—is the final characteristic on my list. The owner may not trade a right away to another individual either for extra helpings of other rights or for money or goods. Such bans fly in the face of the economist's traditional approach to the maximization of welfare. As James Tobin of Yale University put it, "Any good second year graduate student in economics could write a short examination paper proving that voluntary transactions in votes would increase the welfare of the sellers as well as the buyers."[10]

It takes only a little imagination to envision many new markets in rights that might arise if trades were permitted. The ban on indentured service is an obviously coercive limitation on free trade; it discourages investments by businessmen in the training and skills of their employees, and prevents bargains that might be beneficial to both the seller of his person and the buyer. The one-person, one-spouse rule could be altered to permit voluntary exchange by giving each person a marketable ticket to a spouse rather than a nontransferable right to marry one (and no more than one) person at a time. Since jury trials are expensive, society might offer any defendant who waived that right some portion of the savings. Trade in military draft obligations is easy to conceive and, in fact, has occurred in the past. Even the obligation to obey

10. James Tobin, "On Limiting the Domain of Inequality," *Journal of Law and Economics*, Vol. 13 (October 1970), p. 269.

the law might be made marketable, as it was, in a figurative sense, when the Church sold indulgences during the Middle Ages.[11]

In short, the domain of rights is full of infringements on the calculus of economic efficiency. Our rights can be viewed as inefficient, because they preclude prices that would promote economizing, choices that would invoke comparative advantage, incentives that would augment socially productive effort, and trades that potentially would benefit buyer and seller alike.

The Reasons for Rights

Why then does society establish these "inefficient" rights? The justifications for rights take three routes—libertarian, pluralistic, and humanistic.

LIBERTY. To the advocate of laissez-faire, many rights protect the individual citizen against the encroachment of the state, and thus convey benefits that far outweigh any cost of economic inefficiency. Freedom of speech and religion must be universal and unconditional; regulation, limitation, or discrimination with respect to them would vest discretionary authority in the government. Any condition for eligibility to vote that cannot be settled by the presentation of a birth certificate would give powers to some public official who might have an interest in keeping certain people out of the polling booth. Even if a literacy test administered by an objective deity would be desirable, one administered by a bureaucracy would be intolerable. The nice thing about universality and equality is that they are identifiable and objective criteria and hence hard to abuse. Thus, the libertarian embraces equality not because he cares at all for equality but because he cares a great

11. According to the *Encyclopaedia Britannica*, it is a "popular misconception" that an indulgence granted "permission to commit sin." It is suggested instead that "an indulgence can perhaps be best compared to a pardoning of part of the sentence of a prisoner who has performed some good work not directly connected with either his crime or his sentence." By any interpretation, the purchaser of the indulgence was buying some amelioration of the usual workings of holy law.

deal about a limited government whose powers are circumscribed by explicit and objective rules. To him, rights are seen mainly as rights conferred on the individual *against* the state, and this view prevails explicitly regarding individual rights in the marketplace.[12]

This explanation for equally distributed rights can take care of only part of the domain that is in fact defined by existing American institutions. It cannot explain why citizens entrust power to the state to prevent other individuals from encroaching on their freedoms. It cannot explain the whole sphere of civil liberties or public services. Nor can it explain government-imposed bans on the voluntary exchange of rights.

The traditional rationale for public interference with market exchange and for the public provision of services rests on so-called "externalities," which involve the interests of third parties.[13] Environmental regulations are necessary because the pollution of the air and the water by one individual harms innocent bystanders. The production of services for national defense and lighthouses cannot be left to private enterprise because there is no effective way to keep the benefits channeled to the buyers and away from the nonbuyers. No one can be permitted to bargain away his right to call the fire department in return for a tax cut, because his next-door neighbor would be made worse off. While that ban on exchange seems adequately explained by externalities, many of the other bans—for example, that on vote trading—do not.[14] Even

12. See the discussion of various aspects of this issue in F. A. Hayek, *The Constitution of Liberty* (University of Chicago Press, 1960), pp. 85–88, 103–07, 116–17, 153–55.

13. For a classical discussion of externalities, see A. C. Pigou, *The Economics of Welfare* (Macmillan, 1920), pp. 115–16.

14. An interesting (but, to me, unpersuasive) justification of the ban on vote trading as a deterrent to potential monopoly is presented by James M. Buchanan and Gordon Tullock, *The Calculus of Consent* (University of Michigan Press, 1962), pp. 270–74. Their discussion helps to clarify the nature of the externalities in vote trading. Consider the following: If Ann buys Bob's vote, she gains power over Carl, and Carl can be made worse off (or, if Ann is his ally, better off). Hence it is sometimes claimed that an externality exists. But if Ann bought Bob's vote in an auction

with the invocation of externalities, liberty cannot single-handedly explain the full range of rights in American society.

PLURALISM. Another route into the domain of rights, stressing pluralism and diversification, can be sketched along lines developed by my teacher, Karl Polanyi. As he saw it, the network of relationships in a viable society had to rest on a broad base of human motives and human interests. Material gain is (at most) one of the many motives propelling economic activity. In turn, the economy is only one aspect of society and must be "embedded into" a successful society. Polanyi deplored a "market society" in which all other relationships would be subordinated to the marketplace.[15] Rights can then be viewed as a protection against the market domination that would arise if everything could be bought and sold for money. Everyone but an economist knows without asking why money shouldn't buy some things. But an economist has to ask that question. Every asset that lies in the scope of the market is measured by a single yardstick calibrated in dollars. All tradable goods and services are assigned their prices, and their values all become dimensionally comparable: a book is ten loaves of bread or two dozen bottles of beer. The imperialism of the market's

---

market, she would have acquired it only by outbidding Carl—Carl had the opportunity to internalize the cost, and his failure to outbid Ann shows that the benefits to him weren't worth the cost. On the other hand, if the transaction did not take place in an auction market, and Carl had no opportunity to bid, then the welfare cost to him of losing that opportunity has nothing to do with the particular characteristics of votes. If Bob sold Ann strawberries that Carl might have liked to purchase, that would have imposed a welfare cost on him too. Thus, power over a third party is not the correct way to describe the externality. Rather, it arises because of the special feature of votes as tradable commodities—that winner takes all. The swing vote is worth everything, and all others are worth nothing. The value of Carl's vote depends on how the remaining votes are distributed between his allies and opponents. In that sense, any trading between allies and opponents has an external effect on every vote holder who is not engaged in the transaction.

15. Karl Polanyi, "Our Obsolete Market Mentality," in George Dalton (ed.), *Primitive, Archaic, and Modern Economies* (Beacon, 1971), pp. 59–77. Polanyi was not much impressed by the effectiveness of democratic political institutions in circumscribing the domain of the marketplace. Hence, he viewed laissez-faire capitalism as a market society.

valuation accounts for its contribution, and for its threat to other institutions. It can destroy every other value in sight. If votes were traded at the same price as toasters, they would be worth no more than toasters and would lose their social significance.

Society refuses to turn itself into a giant vending machine that delivers anything and everything in return for the proper number of coins. When members of my profession sometimes lose sight of this principle, they invite the nastiest definition of an economist: the person who knows the price of everything and the value of nothing. Society needs to keep the market in its place. The domain of rights is part of the checks and balances on the market designed to preserve values that are not denominated in dollars. For the same reasons that an investor holds many different stocks and bonds in his portfolio, society diversifies its mechanisms for distribution and allocation. It won't put all of its eggs in the market's basket.[16]

One of these mechanisms is the rights bestowed on all the citizens. Another set consists of various nonmonetary distinctions that are awarded unequally in recognition of achievement but that are not allowed to bear price tags. Precisely because they cannot be bought for money, Olympic medals and Phi Beta Kappa keys have special value as motivating forces. Still another set of mechanisms consists of voluntary arrangements among individuals that are based on affection and fraternity. People want friendship and love for "themselves," and not for their money. The bond between friends is not merely bilateral philanthropy nor a mutual-assistance contract. These diversified mechanisms keep the

16. This is the same reasoning that leads to my conviction that real gross national product should not and cannot measure social welfare. See Arthur M. Okun, "Social Welfare Has No Price Tag," *Survey of Current Business,* Vol. 51 (July 1971), Pt. 2, pp. 129–33. In both cases, I am arguing that social welfare is a vector and cannot be adequately described by a scalar. As a result, I am a strong advocate of multidimensional social indicators and a strong opponent of attempts to translate every dimension of social progress and retrogression into a dollar magnitude. That latter endeavor is an act of imperialism by economists, in my judgment.

market in its place and keep society from becoming a giant vending machine. They are the glue that holds society together.

HUMANISM. A third explanation for rights stresses their recognition of the human dignity of all citizens. John Rawls, the Harvard philosopher, has developed that rationale brilliantly, deriving a principle of "equality in the assignment of basic rights and duties"[17] from a theory of the social contract. Rawls asks what kind of a social constitution would be adopted if all the framers of the rules operated in ignorance of their class position in the future society and of their relative standing with respect to assets and abilities. In such an "original position," in Rawls' term, the shared sense of justice as fairness could prevail with no distortion from self-interest, since all participants would be mutually disinterested. He concludes that these founding fathers and mothers would opt for equality in the "basic liberties" that relate to the freedom of the individual to follow his conscience, express his own moral principles, and participate in social decisions.

In Rawls' voluntary association, every member wants to ensure the recognition of the principles of self-respect and of fairness for all citizens, because that recognition protects him. The basic liberties are equally distributed because people value equality as a type of "mutual respect . . . owed to human beings as moral persons."[18] These rights that are obtained without a quid pro quo recognize the worth of every citizen in the society. They go along with membership in the club. They then become the hallmarks of affiliation, a part of human dignity, and take on added significance for that reason. Because they are entitlements and not handouts, people can accept them freely without feeling like freeloaders.

The libertarian, pluralistic, and humanistic explanations of rights are not inconsistent; in modern American society, all three considerations play a role in the domain of rights. The preference

17. John Rawls, *A Theory of Justice* (Harvard University Press, 1971), p. 14 and chap. 4.
18. Ibid., p. 511; see also pp. 60, 250.

for equality à la Rawls is one of the elements underlying the character and the scope of rights. The nature of the rights established by our institutions reveals that equality is one of our social values.

The Scope of Rights

How and where does society draw the boundary lines between the domain of rights and that of the marketplace? It is tempting to say that rights deal with noneconomic assets while the market handles economic assets. But that is circular. Since rights may not be bought and sold for dollars, and since they are distributed freely to citizens, they automatically lack the price-tag hallmark of economic "things." In that sense, rights define and delimit the range of economic assets. The Emancipation Proclamation took human beings off the list of commodities for which the market could set price tags. Less dramatically, if fire departments operated as public utilities and thus charged for their services, they would be viewed in economic terms. Because these services are provided as a right, they are pulled outside the framework of the market. But they nonetheless involve the use of labor and capital; they are paid for collectively through taxation; and their resource costs make them "economic."

To be sure, resource costs influence the boundary line. Any entitlement is more likely to be established as a right when it has relatively low resource costs, when economizing and comparative advantage and the other verities of the marketplace are relatively unimportant compared with the significance of broad sharing and common access.[19] It is much less expensive, in every sense, to fulfill the right to free speech than a "right" to free food. But society does provide some costly or resource-using rights, like public education. And one way proponents of equality seek to narrow the differences in standards of living among Americans is to lengthen

19. Even the dividing line between the trivial "right" of free parking spaces and the economic good of metered parking fits this description. For the former, economizing through a price tag isn't worthwhile.

the list of resource-using rights. A government obligation to provide suitable housing or adequate diets for every citizen would, in effect, set a higher basic minimum of real income for all families. The advocacy of new rights can be carried to extremes. I once got into a heated debate with an audience of medical administrators when, taking what I viewed as an outlandish example, I suggested that any national health program should not grant me at public expense all the pairs of eyeglasses I might like. I learned to my surprise that they favored an unlimited right to eyeglasses.

Economists run into such surprises frequently. Nearly all members of my profession would favor some reliance on "effluent fees"—prices imposed on pollutants—rather than total commitment to complex, detailed regulations, as a means of allocating the safe and tolerable amount of discharge into air and water. But most legislators denounce such proposals as selling licenses to pollute to the rich. Suggestions that stiffer tolls might unclog our highways and bridges get a hostile reception. Arguments that interest rates should be flexible enough to clear financial markets that have ample competition are greeted with derision. Apparently, many public officials and their constituents want these items to be treated as rights and kept out of the marketplace. On a first reaction, I am baffled: When money buys bread and baby's shoes, why should it not buy these things? On second thought, a glimmer of understanding shines through. I think some of the critics are most concerned about extending the list of marketable assets, in general, rather than about including these particular items. They believe the scope of the marketplace is already too great, and they oppose any changes that would add new dimensions of economic inequality.

THE FUZZY RIGHT TO SURVIVAL. While I am not persuaded by the arguments for many proposed new rights, the case for a right to survival is compelling. The assurance of dignity for every member of the society requires a right to a decent existence—to some minimum standard of nutrition, health care, and other essentials of life. Starvation and dignity do not mix well. The principle that the market should not legislate life and death is a cliché. I do not know anyone today who would disagree, in principle, that every person, regardless of merit or ability to pay, should receive medical care and food in the face of serious illness or malnutrition. Attitudes about this issue have changed dramatically during the past century. At least some devotees of laissez-faire capitalism in the nineteenth century opposed in principle any *right* to survival, beyond the right to beg from private philanthropists.[20] To them, economic efficiency required the forceful implementation of the rule that those who do not work shall not eat.

Although the right to survival now seems to be generally accepted, it has not been explicitly written into our statute books. It has been kept fuzzy, because its fulfillment could be very expensive. A formal and clear commitment that individuals could count on would increase the number who call for help. Uncertainty holds down the resource cost. To the needy, help is where they find it. Sometimes, it is found more easily from philanthropic organizations than from public emergency facilities. Sometimes, it is available only through some demeaning proof of dire need—thus imposing a toll of shame in lieu of cash, or a sacrifice of pride for a dinner.

Ever since the days of the New Deal, however, the federal government has increasingly assumed some of these obligations and formalized some commitments. In particular, the right to some

20. Herbert Spencer, for example, wrote in *Social Statics and Man versus the State*, published in 1884: "The command 'if any would not work neither should he eat,' is simply a Christian enunciation of that universal law of Nature under which life has reached its present height—the law that a creature not energetic enough to maintain itself must die. . . ." Spencer was even skeptical of private philanthropy, arguing against the "injudicious charity" that permits "the recipients to elude the necessities of our social existence." These passages are cited in *Introduction to Contemporary Civilization in the West*, A Source Book Prepared by the Contemporary Civilization Staff of Columbia University, Vol. 2 (Columbia University Press, 1946), pp. 553, 555. Polanyi offers other examples of eighteenth and nineteenth century extremism in *The Great Transformation* (Farrar, 1944; Beacon, 1957), pp. 86–118, passim. Rereading the old-time libertarians made me realize how moderate most of the contemporary brand is by comparison.

minimum standard of consumption has been established for the elderly. The evolution of old-age retirement benefits into a right is instructive. The basic philosophy of social security has been and remains contributory, stressing the obligation of people to provide for themselves. Initially, those who had not been covered by the contributory system during their working careers were not entitled to benefits upon their retirement. For the first time, legislation enacted in 1966 bestowed some minimum benefits on all Americans over the age of 72, regardless of whether they had ever contributed to the system. Since then, the level of minimal entitlements has been increased and the age requirement reduced to 65 through additional programs that supplement the standard system of old-age benefits. Currently, the principle of contribution serves mainly to preserve pride while fulfilling the right to survival.[21]

Issues surrounding the extension and implementation of a formal right to a decent existence are the heart of today's controversies about health insurance, the negative income tax, and welfare reform. Fulfilling that right is an urgent and feasible step toward economic equality in America, and I shall discuss that issue in detail in chapter 4.

Rights of survival set floors under the consumption of the various items identified as essential. They thus preserve some incentives for economizing, and leave considerable scope for the marketplace in determining the production and distribution of food, health care, housing, and the like, for the majority of citizens who wish to, and are able to, spend more than the basic minimum that is guaranteed to all. In this respect they differ from free firefighting services, which are essentially unlimited and adequate to serve the needs of virtually all citizens. They also contrast with those political and civil rights that money is not allowed to buy.

---

21. The establishment of old-age payroll-tax "contributions" as mandatory is also interesting. Once society decides it will not let old people starve (regardless of any previous profligacy or imprudence on their part), it cannot realistically permit workers to opt out of the social security system.

BANS ON EXCHANGE. Once political and civil rights are seen as integral to human dignity, it becomes clear why they shouldn't be bought or sold for money. If someone can buy your vote, or your favorable draft number, or a contract for your indentured service, he can buy part of your dignity; he can buy power over you. By prohibiting your sale of rights, society is encroaching on your freedom, but it is also protecting you from others who might want to take your rights away. Your creditors cannot make you part with your dignity. They cannot force you into trades that are made as a last resort, which could not be fair trades and which would be distorted by vast differences in the bargaining power of the participants and by the desperation that spawns them. Any rational person who would sign a contract for indentured service must be in desperate straits. Similarly, anyone taking out a loan to cover basic consumption needs must be operating under extreme pressure; hence the religious bans on usury during the Middle Ages.[22]

Whenever the law bans trades of last resort, it shuts some potential escape valve for the person in desperate straits. In shutting the valve, society implies that there must be better ways of preventing or alleviating that desperation. When, for example, child labor was restricted, widowed mothers and disabled fathers were deprived of the opportunity to make ends meet out of the earnings of their young children. When the battle over child labor was fought in Great Britain, the proponents of the ban viewed it as part of a larger program in which society would provide the disadvantaged with aid in another and better form.[23]

Minimum-wage laws and work-safety legislation can be viewed most fruitfully as further examples of prohibitions on exchanges born of desperation, extending the logic of the ban on indentured service. Some economists strain to understand the sources of

---

22. See Henri Pirenne, *Economic and Social History of Medieval Europe* (Harcourt, Brace, 1937), pp. 137–38.
23. See Pigou, *Economics of Welfare,* pp. 788–90.

minimum-wage laws:[24] Are they justified as an offset to monopoly power in hiring labor? Do they emerge out of a conspiracy by skilled workers to reduce the job opportunities of the unskilled? Or are they urged by the skilled on the premise that wages will be raised all along the line as customary differentials are preserved? Are they well-intentioned but misguided efforts to help the poor? Similarly, some economists wonder whether work-safety legislation is warranted by lack of information about on-the-job dangers.

As I read the laws, they declare that anyone who takes an absurdly underpaid or extremely risky job must be acting out of desperation. That desperation may result from ignorance, immobility, or genuine lack of alternatives, but it should be kept out of the marketplace. Recognizing that objective still leaves plenty of room for debate about the proper scope of these laws. With these bans, society assumes a commitment to provide jobs that are not excessively risky or woefully underpaid. That commitment is often regrettably unfulfilled, and perhaps, if it were fulfilled, the bans would be unnecessary. Still, closing a bad escape valve may be an efficient way of promoting the development of better ones through the political process.

Prohibitions on exchange thus protect a variety of rights and institutions from contamination by the market. But they can also be manipulated to insulate unequal, oppressive, and hierarchical institutions from ventilation by the market. Historically, caste positions, feudal obligations, entailed land, and guild memberships have been maintained among the things that money should not buy and sell. Those bans served to promote inequality as well as economic inefficiency. Indeed, across the spectrum of primitive,

24. A summary of the diverse justifications of economists and others for minimum-wage laws is contained in David E. Kaun, "The Fair Labour Standards Act," *South African Journal of Economics,* Vol. 33 (June 1965), pp. 131–39. For a discussion of the efficacy of minimum-wage laws in alleviating poverty and in offsetting employer control in the labor market, see George J. Stigler, "The Economics of Minimum Wage Legislation," *American Economic Review,* Vol. 36 (June 1946), pp. 358–65.

ancient, medieval, and modern societies, the market has been restricted more often to preserve unequal power and distinction for the few than to guarantee equal rights for the many.[25] Tyrants, warriors, religious zealots, and dictators rarely tolerated the rivalry of the marketplace in their ordered societies. The social consequences of keeping the market in its place can be good or bad, depending on what is put in the other places. The determination to fill many of them with equal rights is a unique characteristic of a democracy.

TRANSGRESSION OF DOLLARS ON RIGHTS

In fact, money can buy a great many things that are not supposed to be for sale in our democracy. Performance and principle contrast sharply. The marketplace transgresses on virtually every right. Money buys legal services that can obtain preferred treatment before the law; it buys platforms that give extra weight to the owner's freedom of speech; it buys influence with elected officials and thus compromises the principle of one person, one vote. The market is permitted to legislate life and death, as evidenced, for example, by infant mortality rates for the poor that are more than one and one-half times those for middle-income Americans.[26]

Even though money generally cannot buy extra helpings of rights directly, it can buy services that, in effect, produce more or better rights. Some kinds of political lobbying, for example, constitute a socially undesirable production process for "counterfeiting"

25. Polanyi's discussions of past social arrangements illustrate this point again and again. But I doubt that he would agree with my generalization. Money arrangements generally get the lowest grades in his evaluation. Charles Kindleberger, a fellow admirer of Polanyi, also notes critically his eagerness to conclude that ". . . interferences in the market economy are justified by the need to preserve the pattern of society and the status of its members." See Charles P. Kindleberger, "The Great Transformation," *Daedalus*, Vol. 103 (Winter 1974), p. 50.

26. Evelyn M. Kitagawa and Philip M. Hauser, *Differential Mortality in the United States: A Study in Socioeconomic Epidemiology* (Harvard University Press, 1973), p. 28.

votes. There are two basic kinds of remedies. One of these countervails the resources available to the rich by providing publicly financed resources to the poor. So long as the rich are able to draw on their own resources, that approach sets a floor without the ceiling needed to achieve *full* equality. The alternative remedy involves upside-down economics—it tries to make the socially undesirable production process less "efficient" so that it becomes more difficult to counterfeit rights. I shall try to illustrate the principles and problems in a few areas.

Equality before the Law

Although it is generally regarded as one of the most sacred rights, equality before the law is often violated. Undoubtedly, the disadvantaged position of the poor before the law stems from many sources; for example, better education and information help affluent people to take full advantage of the legal system as a means of realizing their goals and ambitions. But one element of the disadvantage is readily identifiable, namely, the inequality of representation by lawyers.[27] When a poor defendant comes before the bar of justice accompanied by a public defender or assigned counsel, he clearly has a handicap relative to the wealthy defendant represented by a highly qualified, high-priced lawyer of his choice. Equality before the law deserves a top priority ranking among our rights. To fulfill that right, even minimally, calls for an enormous and costly expansion of legal services for advising and defending the poor.

27. See, for example, Jerome E. Carlin, Jan Howard, and Sheldon L. Messinger, "Civil Justice and the Poor: Issues for Sociological Research," *Law and Society Review*, Vol. 1 (November 1966), pp. 9–90. They point out that "a large proportion of poor defendants (particularly in misdemeanor cases) are not represented at all. Moreover, when counsel is provided he frequently has neither the resources, the skill nor the incentive to defend his client effectively; and he usually enters the case too late to make any real difference in the outcome. Indeed, the generally higher rate of guilty pleas and prison sentences among defendants represented by assigned counsel or the public defender suggest[s] that these attorneys may actually undermine their clients' position . . ." (p. 56).

Money and Political Power

How do large corporations and wealthy individuals throw their weight around unduly in the political process? There is no obvious and natural mechanism that conveys extra helpings of votes to the wealthy—any more than to the good-looking or the especially virtuous. Obviously, one route by which money buys political power is through direct and indirect payments to political decisionmakers. On the best available evidence, most congressmen do not take outright bribes; yet they do seek campaign funds by means that are legal but that nevertheless bestow additional helpings of votes on those who can afford, and who have the interest, to contribute large sums. These contributions have important and pervasive influences on the behavior and attitudes of officials, even of honest and scrupulous officials. I have heard the directors of financing in a campaign organization urge a liberal Democrat to stay away from loophole-closing tax reform as a campaign issue because it would antagonize wealthy potential contributors. Another example was provided by super-rich Howard Hughes, who bought blue chips in the form of a diversified portfolio of campaign contributions to candidates of both parties in an apparent effort to influence particular regional and industrial policies.

CAMPAIGN FINANCING. Full disclosure of contributions is not enough to prevent serious transgression. A drastic limitation on the amount of financial aid that any one individual or organization can give candidates seems essential to equality at the polls. And if large contributors are not allowed to pick up the tab for the opinions and information that should flow in political campaigns, then the taxpayer must. The public financing of campaigns for the Congress and the Presidency is an indispensable ingredient in any satisfactory recipe for reform. And the initial legislative action to provide public financing was the most important law passed in 1974.

To be sure, designing a sound plan for public financing poses tough problems: the taxpayer should not be forced to buy an expensive podium for the vegetarian party, and neither should his funds serve to entrench and rigidify our currently predominant two parties. But, as I read the arguments against public financing, the real controversy is fundamental.[28] Opponents of public financing want primarily to preserve the freedom of individuals to spend their money, if and as they choose, in order to influence the outcome of elections. In my view, that is something money should not buy. Thus, society must erect a sign that clearly says "no trespassing" on the right of universal suffrage.

Restrictions on campaign contributions can reduce significantly the political power of the super-rich. Of course, some of the wealthy will find ways to defy the spirit of the law by selling the congressman products at a discount, by hiring his nephew, and by developing dodges that are far more ingenious than any I could possibly concoct. But, if necessary, the law against bribes can be clarified and extended. And limitations on contributions help to unmask some types of payments that have been explained away as "campaign assistance."

LOBBYING. Restricting contributions will still leave people and corporations many ways to show the intensity of their feelings about issues and candidates. Some of these ways are good for the process of deliberation; some are bad; some are questionable. And all involve some expenditures of money: even a letter to a congressman takes a postage stamp. The key questions in appraising the legitimacy of lobbying activities are: How does the lobbyist make his case for or against proposed policy actions? What are his instruments of persuasion?

As a means by which people (and business firms, unions, and associations) can show *how much* they care about particular political decisions, lobbying is a legitimate—indeed, valuable—input in the political process. And that includes promises and threats

---

28. See, for example, the arguments in Ralph K. Winter, Jr., in association with John R. Bolton, *Campaign Financing and Political Freedom* (American Enterprise Institute, 1973).

about how the pleaders will vote in the next election. Lobbying is also a legitimate way to convey evidence about the favorable or unfavorable consequences for the nation of a particular bill or executive action. Of course, much of the evidence will be self-serving. Some briefs I have seen written by economists, predicting that a certain action will give us heaven or hell, just couldn't represent the earnest professional judgment of the authors. But the safeguards against such pleading must lie in the good sense (and informed skepticism) of the public official and in stronger professional codes of ethics, rather than in laws to ban unsound or insincere argumentation.

Lobbying is intolerable when the means of persuasion are promises of direct or indirect payments of a pecuniary character (money, gifts, job patronage, honoraria, and the like) in return for the official's decision. Much of lobbying has been linked to the promise of campaign contributions, and restrictions on the latter should help to reduce *some* of the worst lobbying pressures. Beyond that, a code of conduct is needed to establish the boundaries of fair relationships between legislators and executive officials, on the one hand, and lobbying groups, on the other. For one thing, that code ought to keep any former public official out of the lobbying game for several years after leaving office, thus precluding the temptation to build good will as an investment for future employment.

If the uses of fat checkbooks in the political process can be tightly regulated, the plutocracy will lose much of its political punch. The captains and giants of industry are a tiny part of the electorate, and they are reined in by the public's natural skepticism about, and antagonism against, their particular interests and pleadings. The majority of the folks back home tend to believe that what's good for General Motors *can't* be good for the country, and that gives a congressman incentives to oppose publicly positions advocated by General Motors. Indeed, as the wealthy see it, knee-jerk populism gives them an unfair handicap in national debates. I would guess that it comes close to evening the score.

It is harder to even the score in cases where the wealthy have subtle influences on groups of middle-class voters. Employees, stockholders, suppliers, and neighbors of large corporations may become dependent on them and hence become exponents of positions favored by the rich and the powerful. These interdependencies arise because the American economy does not fit the textbook's purely competitive model in which everybody has the option of taking an alternative job that is virtually as good as the one he holds, or the option of selling to an alternative customer willing to buy the product at the going price. The interests of stockholders of multinational companies were furthered by U.S. government actions to undercut the Chilean socialist regime that sought to expropriate Anaconda and ITT. Employees of the steel industry have interests in curbs on imported steel, even when such measures are bad for labor on the whole. To the extent that these are the genuine interests of the small stockholders and the workers, their expression in the political process is perfectly appropriate. On the other hand, through the subtle dependencies of many average Americans on them, the wealthy can obtain undue political leverage.

Consider a hypothetical example. The vice president of a large manufacturing corporation walks into the office of a congressman whose district is plagued by high unemployment. The corporate representative explains that his firm is contemplating the construction of a plant in the congressman's district, and is investigating the various aspects of that location decision. Naturally, the firm wants to know the climate of the district to estimate heating bills, and similarly it wants to assess the political climate. It is not unreasonable to ask whether the firm is going to be represented by a friendly congressman who will view its interests sympathetically. The congressman is tempted to pledge his friendship and help, perhaps solely to protect the interests of his constituents in the availability of good jobs. Although nobody is doing anything wrong, I find something wrong with this picture. And yet I cannot prescribe a code of conduct that would distinguish clearly between right ways and wrong ways for legislators to pursue the interests of their constituents in their relationships with big business.

Similar problems arise from the power of interest groups that have large memberships and therefore control many votes. Independent oil producers, farmers, teachers, homebuilders, unionized workers, and welfare recipients all have organizations in Washington working to pass or oppose some laws. So do various groups with particularly strong avocational interests, like gun enthusiasts and the owners of private aircraft. Not all of these groups are rich, but they all have focused objectives. They will support or oppose vigorously a candidate according to his stand on the particular issues close to their hearts. Intensity of preferences is the name of their game; and it is a legitimate game, intended to balance the inherent bias of democracy in favor of actions that benefit the majority a little even when they hurt a small minority a great deal.[29]

Yet these groups seem to tilt the balance in the other direction, often obtaining benefits for the relatively few they represent at the expense of the unorganized majority. Their power is enhanced by the costliness of information about the legislative process. Only the rare milk consumer knows how his congressman votes on dairy price supports, but every milk producer does. But voter-organizing and voter-informing are usually reinforced by candidate-funding. In their repeated efforts to raise dairy support prices during the late sixties and early seventies, the associations of milk producers did not rely exclusively on their ability to marshal the votes of their members; they threw in the secret ingredient of large campaign contributions. The Watergate revelations about dollar-enriched milk products help to clarify why 200,000 milk producers have usually beaten 200,000,000 milk consumers in the political process.

---

29. This point is argued strongly by Buchanan and Tullock, *Calculus of Consent;* see, for example, p. 127.

CONSUMER POWER. When money transgresses equal political rights, the consumer most often is the victim. Some of the remedies lie in strengthening the countervailing power of the consumer against the producer. Voluntary associations of consumers have grown in strength during the past decade; and, on balance, I believe they have been constructive. Occasionally, articulate consumer advocates have pushed through legislation that most American consumers did not want, like the mandatory interlock ignition system, but they have been promptly reversed.[30] And Congress has realized that no single person speaks for the consumer.

The proposed Consumer Protection Agency—a publicly financed office of consumer advocacy—is one worthwhile step to strengthen the public's power. The bill to create that agency was brutally filibustered to death in 1974, but it should come alive in the near future.

At the local level, opening a line of communication for the individual to his government through a personal representative—the ombudsman system—is an appealing way to help fulfill the rights to public services. As the husband of a part-time ombudsperson, I have been regaled with anecdotes about services performed by the government of the District of Columbia in response to telephone calls from citizens. Often the expression of appreciation that follows seems out of proportion to the specific mission accomplished; the fulfillment of the person's request is especially valuable as a demonstration that rights can be validated. In addition, such a system gives the top local officials a useful tally of the public's specific complaints and concerns.

The Corrective Strategy

My purpose is not to advance specific remedies, but to highlight the general problem of transgression as an urgent one that

---

30. I also regret that consumer advocates pay so little attention to the harm imposed on consumers by anticompetitive laws, like barriers to imports, resale price maintenance, and the like. I suppose it is harder to dramatize these damaging institutions than to expose unsafe products or false advertising.

requires a serious and concerted attack by political scientists, lawyers, economists, and the public at large. Some transgressions of money on rights make a mockery of America's commitment to civil liberties and democracy. Some of our most cherished rights are auctioned off to the highest bidder. These transgressions may be as important a source of cynicism, radicalism, and alienation as the vast disparities in material living standards between rich and poor. Yet pitifully little effort has gone into devising measures that would narrow the gap between principle and practice.

The key remedies must be specific aids and sanctions rather than general efforts to curb bigness and wealth. Breaking a $20 billion corporation into ten $2 billion pieces still leaves entities large enough to transgress political rights, if such actions are tolerated by the law. Even if the most ambitious program of progressive taxation were enacted, Howard Hughes would retain more than enough money to produce counterfeit votes. It is no easy task to formulate and enforce specific and detailed rules of the game that would prevent him from spending money to acquire undue power. But I find that route far more promising than one that seeks to curb his power by taking his money away. The case for progressive taxation rests on other grounds, which I shall discuss in chapter 4.

In some limited ways, restrictions on the scope of economic activities by the wealthy may help to curb their power. The more markets a corporation operates in and the more congressional districts it provides jobs and orders for, the greater the opportunities for the plutocrats to obtain undue political power. In this respect, conglomerate corporations like ITT are perhaps the most dangerous ones. In retrospect, the conglomerate merger movement deserved more attention than it received from many economists, who viewed it complacently because it did not reduce the extent of competition within industries. A more determined effort to limit size and scope can thus help a little. But the basic transgressions of the marketplace on equal rights must be curbed by specific, detailed rules on what money should not buy.

Even so, transgression cannot be totally eliminated. Money will still impinge to some degree because that undesirable production process will retain some efficiency in producing counterfeit rights. In that sense, it seems impossible to achieve Rawls' "lexical ordering,"[31] which insists that equality in the domain of basic liberties should never be compromised by inequality of other assets. Thus, I cannot quarrel with the radical's verdict that complete equality is unattainable in anything unless it is attained in everything. But if the transgression problem is approached with less-than-perfectionist objectives, the outlook is much brighter. The thousand-dollar-a-day lawyer need not be a grave threat if adequate public defenders are available. The opportunity for a wealthy individual to take advertising space in the newspaper to expound his views on social issues is no great encroachment on the freedom of speech of others. Buying advertising space is tolerable; buying legislators is intolerable. I am hopeful that a concerted and focused program of specific remedies can correct the serious transgressions of dollars on the domain of rights, and I am convinced that the construction of such a program should be the top priority for social reformers.

31. Rawls, *Theory of Justice*, pp. 302–03.

CHAPTER TWO

THE CASE FOR THE MARKET

U nlike the equal rights discussed in chapter 1, the economic
institutions of the United States rest on voluntary exchange
and on private ownership of productive assets; and they involve
money rewards and penalties that generate an unequal distribution of income and wealth. Thus the anatomy of the American
economy contrasts sharply with the egalitarian structure of its pol-
ity. At the same time, the functioning—indeed, the very life—of
the market depends on the coercive powers of political institutions. The state uses these powers to establish and ensure rights
in the marketplace, directly supply some essential services, and
indirectly generate the environment of trust, understanding, and
security that is vital to the daily conduct of business.

WHY CAPITALISM?

Our economic institutions are precariously perched on the will—
or the whim—of the body politic. Neither rights to ownership of
any class of physical assets nor rights to after-tax income are given
constitutional safeguards; in principle, they could be curbed drastically by a vote of 51 percent of the elected representatives of
the public. And a majority could easily wish to curb them drastically. The bottom half of all American families has only about

31

one-twentieth of all wealth and roughly a quarter of all income.[1] How then does capitalism survive in a democracy? What makes the not-so-affluent majority so charitable toward the rich minority? For one thing, those on the low end of the economic totem pole do not have identical interests on many issues; elderly white rural ex-sharecroppers, young black urban welfare mothers, and middle-aged low-wage janitorial workers would find it hard to unite behind a particular program of redistribution. Nonetheless, the tolerance of the masses for economic inequality is puzzling.

At least, it is to me. It does not puzzle some radicals, who see the basic explanation in the transgressions of dollars on rights. According to that argument, because money buys votes, democracy is a sham. Because money controls the media, people are misinformed; hence, their votes fail to express their true economic interests. Thus, both economic and political power remain concentrated in the same minority, which perpetuates oppression and inequality.[2]

Nor does the question puzzle some of the most ardent enthusiasts for the marketplace. They have a ready package of reasons why a rational citizen—rich or poor—should support capitalism. That package highlights the contribution of a decentralized market economy to personal freedom. It may also include an ethical defense for wide income differentials that reflect differences in productive contribution. It features the superior efficiency of a market economy. Compared with any alternative system, American capitalism provides higher standards of living for most families, even though some live better than others. Fortunately, it is argued, most voters recognize their true interests and do not behave like the dog in the manger.

1. Sources and concepts for data on income and wealth distribution are discussed in footnotes to chapter 3.

2. See, for example, Arthur Lothstein (ed.), *"All We Are Saying . . .": The Philosophy of the New Left* (Putnam, 1970): ". . . established forms of representative and parliamentary democracy . . . serve only to legitimize the economic hegemony of the ruling class, and to perpetuate class politics. . . . power which has been usurped by the ruling class . . . is wielded by [the ruling class] for the twin purposes of economic self-aggrandizement and political domination" (p. 15).

The limited evidence available from surveys of public opinion and attitudes suggests that Archie Bunker's preference for capitalism rests on grounds similar to those of the intellectual protagonists for the market. (I will not try to infer who is influencing whom.) In one recent survey, a 28-year-old lower-class woman from Boston offered a rather typical declaration of attitudes toward an equal distribution of income: "It's communism—everybody is the same and they all share. I wouldn't want it. If I work harder than somebody else, why should I share or . . . why shouldn't I be able to . . . live better. . . ?"[3] In particular, people show surprisingly little resentment toward the extremely wealthy.[4] While they express some concern about inequalities of opportunity and discriminatory treatment, most view those aspects as flaws rather than fundamental defects of the system.

More generally, the public displays deep-seated conservatism toward any major economic reform. People fear the unknown; they know what they have; and they have much to lose besides their alleged chains. Moreover, public criticism or even discussion of income inequality is rare, perhaps because differences in incomes arise so naturally. In the process of producing goods and services, the market also grinds out a set of wage, interest, and profit rates that determine the incomes of the participants. The production and distribution aspects are separated in economic analysis, but not in economic life. Production and income come out of the same machine, much as light and heat emanate from the sun. Except for the occasions when people reach for sunglasses or the air conditioning switch, they do not perceive the two separate aspects of sunshine either.

When either laymen or experts discuss the unequal rewards and penalties generated by a market economy, three aspects are stressed frequently—the link to freedom, the fairness of rewards,

3. Lee Rainwater, *What Money Buys: Inequality and the Social Meanings of Income* (Basic Books, 1974), p. 168.
4. Ibid., pp. 170–74.

and the incentives of differential incomes for enhancing efficiency. I shall examine and evaluate those three issues in turn.

RIGHTS AND FREEDOMS IN THE MARKETPLACE

While society bans exchanges in many social and political areas, it protects options to trade and to earn and spend money in the marketplace. It establishes the rights of citizens to acquire income by selling the services of their labor and capital, and to dispose of income by buying goods and services from others. By some standards, these rights in the marketplace represent universal and equal rights to earn unequal incomes. Moreover, the rights of citizens to pick their jobs and to select the items for their market baskets, at least out of some reasonable menu of options, are essential elements of personal freedom.

Property Rights and Freedom

The boundaries around these rights, however, raise intriguing and controversial issues. My right to pick my job is restricted in many ways. I cannot sell heroin, pornography that lacks redeeming social value, letter-delivery or telephone services, nor, given my particular training, legal or medical services. Each of these restrictions is controversial, because people have vastly different attitudes about the importance of various liberties and of other values. To me, the fact that anyone without medical training cannot sell health-care services is sensible protection for consumers; to Milton Friedman, it is undesirable coercion.[5]

The scope of private property raises even sharper controversies. In order to permit individuals to trade, the law must define a right to private property; I need to know what I own and what I can sell. Thus, the law must establish a division between private

5. Milton Friedman, *Capitalism and Freedom* (University of Chicago Press, 1962), p. 158.

and collective ownership.[6] The big question is where to draw the line. According to one answer, the broadest possible scope of private property is the best, because it offers the broadest range of individual choice, and thus maximum personal freedom. That line of reasoning follows from John Locke's conception of physical property as an extension of the individual—an instrument that broadens his or her scope for action.

Such a conception may have seemed natural in a world of yeomen farmers;[7] but it loses meaning in a modern industrial society that rests heavily on wealth in the form of paper claims to assets that owners do not use directly. Stocks and bonds make their owners wealthier and more secure; but they cannot be consumed as such nor do they enhance the productivity of the owner's labor. Obviously, they enlarge the freedom to acquire, own, and exchange property; but that is all they do for freedom. Also, much modern property consists of creatures of the state, in the sense that it could not be owned in a Robinson Crusoe world. Our government fabricates property out of thin air when it originates patents and copyrights, broadcasting licenses, taxi medallions, and common-carrier certificates. It creates the joint-stock corporation and invests it with many of the legal rights and privileges of a human being, even though no corporation has ever been observed walking, talking, or courting a corporation of the opposite sex. Such government-created institutions are extremely useful, but encroachment by the government on them should hardly inspire a freedom march. If they are extensions of the individual and of personal freedoms, they must be long-distance hookups.

Indeed, from another point of view, the keep-off sign can be viewed as a pervasive encroachment on personal freedom. The ownership of property by one individual deprives 200,000,000

6. See the discussion in F. A. Hayek, *The Constitution of Liberty* (University of Chicago Press, 1960), pp. 140–42.

7. See the discussion in R. H. Tawney, *The Acquisitive Society* (Harcourt, Brace and Howe, 1920), pp. 58–62.

nonowners of access to that asset. To evaluate the net gain in freedom provided by private ownership (rather than public access)
for any asset requires a balancing of pluses and minuses. The
plus is the enhanced scope of the owner through exclusive powers over the asset; the minus is the restriction the keep-off sign
imposes on nonowners. In some instances, the verdict is clear-cut.
R. H. Tawney, the British egalitarian, reminds his readers: "In the
past, human beings, roads, bridges and ferries, civil, judicial and
clerical offices, and commissions in the army have all been private property."[8] In such cases, collectivized ownership enhanced
freedom. And the collectivization of toothbrushes, clothing, and
one-family homes would impair freedom. To each his own is a
sensible rule for such cases, which fit the Lockean mold. Similarly,
small businesses and family farms can be fitted into that mold;
they are extensions of their owners, and that fact helps to explain
the political enthusiasm they engender.

It is even harder to appraise the freedom issue for the many
places in modern industrial society where private ownership does
not entail exclusivity and public ownership does not provide public
access. American stockholders in privately owned steel companies
must heed the keep-off signs posted by management as carefully
as those who do not own stock. Moreover, their opportunities to
control the assets of which they are part owners are sharply limited. But by the same token, British citizens have no more rights of
access or control in their (on-again, off-again) nationalized steel
industry. An appeal to liberty cannot settle the merits of private
ownership of steel. In another case, private owners of U.S. restaurants and hotels have recently lost the legal authority to exclude
any citizen for virtually any reason other than his inability or
unwillingness to pay the posted price. The encroachment on the
freedom of the owners enhanced the freedom of the potentially

8. Ibid., p. 73.

excluded customers; I defy anyone to tell me whether the net change in freedom is positive or negative.[9]

If a foundation offered me a $10 million grant to develop empirical tests of the proposition that government ownership of large parks or airlines or oil companies decreases (or increases) freedom, I would have no idea where to begin spending the money. Yet some people argue the case for private ownership of such items as though it were the same kind of basic liberty as freedom of speech or universal suffrage. The case for private ownership of productive assets must rest primarily on efficiency, as I hope to show below.

not freedom

Transgression by the State

There is another link between the marketplace and freedom that seems stronger to me.[10] A market economy helps to safeguard political rights against encroachment by the state. Private ownership and decisionmaking circumscribe the power of the government—or, more accurately, of those who run the government—and hence its ability to infringe on the domain of rights.

In the polar case of a fully collectivized economy, political rights would be seriously jeopardized. If the government commanded all the productive resources of the society, it could suppress dissent, enforce conformity, and snuff out democracy. As an entry on some of the "enemies lists" compiled by Nixon aides, I shudder in imagining my income and status during that era if

9. For an effort to deal with such issues of freedom that I find interesting but unacceptable, see Thomas G. Moore, "An Economic Analysis of the Concept of Freedom," *Journal of Political Economy,* Vol. 77 (July/August 1969), Pt. 1, pp. 532–44.

10. My first and second links are analogous to Milton Friedman's distinction between the contribution of a market economy to economic freedom, and its indirect contribution to political freedom. That potentially useful distinction makes me uncomfortable, however, because the dividing line between "economic freedom" and "political freedom" depends on where society draws the boundary between the domain of dollars and that of rights. See Friedman, *Capitalism and Freedom,* pp. 7–14.

the federal government had been the only employer. That ardent exponent of laissez-faire, Friedrich Hayek, quotes approvingly a brief passage from the disillusioned communist Leon Trotsky: "In a country where the sole employer is the State, opposition means death by slow starvation. The old principle, who does not work shall not eat, has been replaced by a new one: who does not obey shall not eat."[11] I cherish this rare occasion when I can agree with both Hayek and Trotsky!

Similarly, a free press could not be financed adequately or operated securely in a totally collectivized economy. Our present economic system generates some supply of dissent and criticism. It has room for Seymour Hersh to expose My Lai in the *New York Times* and for Bob Woodward and Carl Bernstein to unlock the mystery of Watergate in the *Washington Post*. That imperfect market is far better than none at all, and better than a system in which investigative journalism would get into print only on clandestine mimeograph machines.

The transgression on rights by the bureaucracy is a serious and worrisome problem. But a shrinkage of the power of the state to microscopic size is neither necessary nor sufficient to eliminate the problem. The compelling case against the socialization of *Time* and the *New York Times* is not an argument for little rather than big government within the currently relevant range. The bugging of journalists, the extra-legal police forces, and other abuses of executive power during the Nixon years could have been perpetrated just as easily if the federal budget had been $100 billion rather than $300 billion. The punitive use of audits by the Internal Revenue Service against political enemies would have been just as tempting if federal income tax rates had been half their present level. In chapter 1, I expressed my doubts that the transgression on rights by plutocrats could be significantly reduced simply by redistribution of their income and wealth; for similar reasons, I

11. Hayek, *Constitution of Liberty*, p. 137.

am convinced that rights cannot be satisfactorily protected from transgression by bureaucrats simply through shrinkage of the size and scope of government.

If federal economic power grew and grew, it might ultimately become impossible to restrict its uses and prevent it from encroaching on rights. But it is hard to judge where that danger point might lie. Scandinavian governments have wielded tremendous economic power without compromising democratic institutions. On the other hand, Fascist governments have oppressed political opponents while maintaining a private-enterprise economy. As compared with the polar extreme of total economic centralization, a market economy clearly does protect rights from transgression by the state. That is a highly relevant consideration in evaluating proposals for dramatic increases in centralization. It is impressive that the history of nations with fully collectivized economies reveals not a single free election nor one free press.

THE ETHICS OF REWARDS

Some conservatives would argue that, if a market economy is functioning properly, people simply get out of it what they put into it. And the resulting differences in income are acceptable and fair—perhaps even ideal. Fair games have losers as well as winners. Rights in the marketplace do not guarantee anyone an income, but then freedom of speech does not guarantee anyone an audience. By this reasoning, fair and equal treatment is provided by the opportunity to induce people to pay for services—just as it is by the opportunity to induce people to listen.

Reward for Contribution

With a sprinkling of appropriate assumptions, it can be demonstrated that a competitive market will pay workers and investors the value of their contributions to output. This so-called marginal productivity theory of distribution is the economist's formal way of saying that you take out what you put in. The fruits of labor and capital are converted into dollars and given back to the suppliers. At the turn of this century, that theory of distribution was greeted by some social thinkers as divine revelation of the justice of a competitive economy.[12] Today, however, economists do not invoke the name of the Lord in support of the market. In fact, most of the ardent supporters of the market explicitly reject the claim that distribution in accordance with marginal productivity is necessarily just distribution.[13]

Nonetheless, the ethical appeal of reward for contribution remains very much alive and shows up in subtle ways. When authors distinguish between the deserving and undeserving poor, or the deserving and undeserving rich; when Marxists challenge marginal productivity with a theory that attributes all value to labor input, directly or indirectly; or when egalitarian economists rest their case for altering the verdict of the market on allegedly scientific comparisons of the "utility" of income to different people, they are all paying homage—as supporters or detractors—to the initial presumption that income ought to be based on contribution to output.

Therefore, it is worth exploring the ways contributions are rewarded in the marketplace and evaluating the system of rewards in terms of ethical standards. To begin with, the actual pricing of productive services differs from the textbook results of a competitive model in a dozen ways. I will mention only a few. When there is "monopsony"—monopoly power on the buyer's side—in

12. For a discussion of this view as set forth by John Bates Clark, see M. Blaug, *Economic Theory in Retrospect* (Irwin, 1962), pp. 403–08; also John Rawls, *A Theory of Justice* (Harvard University Press, 1971), pp. 308–09.

13. See, for example, Frank H. Knight, *The Ethics of Competition and Other Essays* (Harper, 1935), pp. 54–58; and Hayek, *Constitution of Liberty*, pp. 93–100. Friedman is the exception: he does not reject (nor does he embrace) the ethics of reward for contribution; see *Capitalism and Freedom*, pp. 161–65. For a contrasting position, see Lester Thurow, "Toward a Definition of Economic Justice," *Public Interest*, No. 31 (Spring 1973), p. 72.

the labor market, the employer may be able to pay workers less than they contribute. Even without monopsony, most markets for labor and capital lack the auction system needed to ensure an equilibrium wage or price that avoids shortages and excess supplies. Moreover, the contributions of two factors that must operate together—like two men on a two-handled saw—cannot always be assessed separately. Finally, as John Kenneth Galbraith has emphasized, the contribution of workers is often judged and their pay set by managers who have interests and objectives of their own, quite distinct from the profitability of their firm.[14]

Sources of Productive Contribution

The deviations from the competitive model are serious and significant; yet, I believe, still more fundamental issues about income rewards arise even in the unreal and ideal world of that model. What determines the competitive market value of the services of any citizen? Are the resulting rewards really fair?

The productive contribution of the services I could sell in a hypothetical competitive market depends on four sets of elements: (1) the skills and assets that I have acquired through my lifetime; (2) the abilities and talents with which I was born; (3) the effort I am willing to expend; and (4) the supply and demand situations for other services related to the ones I can offer.

ACQUIRED ASSETS. What I have to sell today reflects my entire life history, including the nutrition and health care I have received, my education, my previous job experience, and any physical property I have acquired by previous saving or inheritance. To the extent that my current supply of marketable services is augmented by effort (or thrift) that I have exercised previously, I am reaping the harvest from the seeds I planted in the past. But to the extent that my present position reflects heavily the advantages of family background, or privilege, or status, I am reaping what others have sown.

---

14. *The New Industrial State* (Houghton Mifflin, 1967), pp. 124–35.

To switch metaphors, some of the contestants get a head start while others have handicaps. Social and economic disparities among families make the race unfair. The importance of the uneven positions at the starting line and the possibilities of making the race fairer are complex and controversial issues to which I will return in chapter 3. But it seems undeniable in principle that the prizes for performance would be more defensible ethically if everyone had an even start.

NATURAL ABILITIES. Those who shrug their shoulders at the social and economic differences in starting positions emphasize the differences in natural abilities. They argue that these biological differences are even more important. It isn't capitalism's fault that infants differ in endowments at the starting line of birth and even of conception. Such differential talents are, by definition, hereditary rather than environmental; they are given to the individual by his parents rather than developed or earned by him. Thus they preclude truly fair starts.[15] Should everyone therefore stop running races? Obviously not. In real track meets, no official has ever disqualified a runner for having "fast genes." The non-shoulder-shrugger retorts that society should aim to ameliorate, and certainly not to compound, the flaws of the universe. It cannot stop rain, but it does manufacture umbrellas. Similarly, it can decide to restrict prizes that bestow vastly higher standards of living on people with greater acquired assets or greater innate abilities. With tongue in cheek, Henry Simons of the University of Chicago once developed a tantalizing case for reversing the income distribution: the talented are unavoidably favored by being more talented; giving them higher incomes compounds their accidental and unmerited advantages.[16] John Rawls' tongue was not in his cheek when he stated his "principle of redress": "to provide genuine equality

15. Frank H. Knight, *Risk, Uncertainty and Profit* (Houghton Mifflin, 1921), pp. 374–75; see also Friedman, *Capitalism and Freedom*, p. 164.
16. Henry C. Simons, *Personal Income Taxation* (University of Chicago Press, 1938), pp. 12–13.

of opportunity, society must give more attention to those with fewer native assets and to those born into the less favorable social positions."[17] Indeed, the principle of redress is a common feature of family life, where extraordinary efforts are often devoted to the education and happiness of handicapped children. Fairness is clearly not interpreted as reward for contribution in such cases.

EFFORT. Differences in incomes that are associated with differences in effort are generally regarded as fair. If everyone were offered the same hourly wage rate and the opportunity to work as many hours as he or she chose, the resulting discrepancies on payday would be understandable. In fact, it would seem unfair for the person who takes more leisure to get just as much income. Leisure is a form of income and an element in one's standard of living; thus, a sacrifice of leisure must be compensated in other ways if fairness is to be achieved.[18]

Extra income for extra effort is unquestionably useful in providing incentives as well as fair compensation for parting with leisure. The two roles are hard to disentangle. When the fairness issue is viewed in a broad and searching context, some difficult questions arise. Shouldn't society be capable of tolerating diverse individual attitudes toward work and leisure? Would society really want to starve those who might conceivably have lazy genes? Suppose for a moment that incentives are not relevant. If the total input of effort were completely unaffected, would society want the beachcomber to eat less well than his fellow citizens, including others who do not work, such as children, the elderly, and students on fellowships?

Nor is it obvious, in that broader perspective, that incentives for effort to produce marketable output should take the form principally of purchasing power over marketable output. In a Robinson Crusoe economy, the individual putting forth the effort must

17. Rawls, *Theory of Justice*, p. 100.
18. The same is true about risky, unpleasant, or exhausting work; I shall say more about this range of issues in chapter 3.

get the resulting output. But other societies can provide different kinds of incentives. Many primitive societies allowed those who shirked work to eat just as well as workers,[19] but some insisted that the nonworker eat apart from the rest of the community and others had ceremonies in which the well-fed slacker was publicly scorned by his brother-in-law. When the advanced capitalist economy provides its incentives for productive effort primarily in dollars, that revives the Robinson Crusoe arrangement with the innovation of a monetary system. Should that be viewed as progress or retrogression?

RELATED SUPPLIES AND DEMANDS. The value of my marginal product does not depend solely on my skills and effort. It can be altered greatly by changes in the behavior of other people, even though I keep doing the same old thing no better and no worse than ever. If more economists emerge who are willing to make speeches, or if audiences lose interest in talks given by economists, that would be bad news for my income. But would I then really be less productive? Would I deserve a drop in income? Is it ethically (as distinct from pragmatically) desirable for incomes to rest on the shifting sands of technology and tastes?

In view of those dependencies on other people, the concept of my contribution to output becomes hazy. Production comes out of a complex, interdependent system and may not be neatly attributable to individual contributors. Henry Ford's mass-produced automobile was a great success in a country with a high average income, three thousand miles for unimpeded driving, an alert and ambitious work force, and a government that could protect travelers and enforce rules of the road. It would have been a loser in Libya. In that sense, most production processes involve "joint inputs," like the two-handled saw.[20] That aspect is recognized in

19. Karl Polanyi, "Our Obsolete Market Mentality," in George Dalton (ed.), *Primitive, Archaic, and Modern Economies* (Beacon, 1971), pp. 65–67.
20. In viewing the whole social and political system as an "input," I am using an unconventional—but nonetheless relevant—concept of joint inputs.

a few private arrangements, which reward teams rather than individuals. The same World Series shares are given to Johnny Bench and the bench-warming third-string catcher, even though their salaries during the regular season are vastly different. Would it be a desirable innovation for some portion of the social output to be shared equally by all the players, like a World Series kitty?

In fact, if everyone received the full measure of his marginal product and no joint inputs existed, the economic benefits generated by great entrepreneurs and inventors would accrue entirely to them. There would then be no "trickle-down" of progress to the masses.[21] Benefits do actually trickle down precisely because the big winners do not obtain—or at least do not maintain—the full rewards for their contribution to improved technology, increased knowledge, and accumulated capital. The trickle-down of benefits is a merit of capitalism in the real world, and it works insofar as the distribution of income departs from the strict standard of reward for personal contribution to production.

Varying Verdicts

I have dozens of good questions about the fairness of market-determined incomes. But I don't claim to have any good answers. The appraisal is obviously a matter of personal judgment. In mine, incomes that match productivity have no ethical appeal. Equality in the distribution of incomes (allowing for voluntary leisure as a form of income) as well as in the distribution of rights would be my ethical preference. Abstracting from the costs and the consequences, I would prefer more equality of income to less and would like complete equality best of all. This preference is a simple

---

21. The formal analysis of trickle-down may be viewed along the following lines: Consider capital-deepening without technical change. The profit rate is driven down over time; and rent on previously invested capital is lowered to match the marginal product of new capital. Then benefits trickle down from the "old" capitalists. The marginal product of labor is raised by capital-deepening, so workers get the benefits of the trickle.

extension of the humanistic basis for equal rights. To extend the domain of rights and give every citizen an equal share of the national income would give added recognition to the moral worth of every citizen, to the mutual respect of citizens for one another, and to the equivalent value of membership in the society for all.[22]

Nonetheless, my preference for one person, one income, is not nearly so strong as that for one person, one vote. Equality in material welfare has much lower benefits and far higher costs than equality of political and civil entitlements. Perhaps because material objects do not seem all-important, it is far less invidious to deprive some citizens of automobiles than to deprive them of the right to vote or freedom of religion. Second, while the provision of equal political and civil rights often imposes costs on society (as I noted in chapter 1), the attempt to enforce equality of income would entail a much larger sacrifice. In pursuing such a goal, society would forgo any opportunity to use material rewards as incentives to production. And that would lead to inefficiencies that would be harmful to the welfare of the majority. Any insistence on carving the pie into equal slices would shrink the size of the pie. That fact poses the tradeoff between economic equality and economic efficiency. Insofar as inequality does serve to promote efficiency in ways that I will discuss below, I can accept some measure of it as a practicality. I can live with rules of the game that make it fair not to share—just as that lady from Boston insisted. But that is a feature of the universe that I regret rather than enjoy.

Many in our society, including some losers as well as most winners, seem to enjoy the rules of the game and the contest. They cheer loudly for success in the marketplace, and reinforce income incentives by vesting those who succeed with social status. The

22. I regard this Rawlsian basis for egalitarianism as far sounder than a foundation based on interdependent utilities or interpersonal comparisons of utility. R. H. Tawney had the same idea: ". . . because men are men, social institutions . . . should . . . emphasize and strengthen . . . the common humanity which unites them . . ." See *Equality* (5th ed., London: Allen & Unwin, 1964), p. 49.

marketplace becomes a great American game; the winners are made proud and the losers embarrassed. The widespread mental depression that accompanied economic depression among the chronically unemployed of the thirties, the satisfaction derived by those who "make it" into the economic mainstream, and the bourgeois aspirations of the poor all reveal the deeply ingrained market ethic of American society.[23] In a sense, these attitudes preserve some of the features of the primitive societies that invoke ceremonies to penalize the lazy and reward the energetic.

Those who enjoy the game seem particularly fascinated by jackpot prizes. The possibility of "making it big" seems to motivate many Americans, including some who have not made it at all. They dream of rags-to-riches and project that dream from generation to generation. There are enough examples of winners to keep it alive and to encourage education, saving, and bourgeois values. In 1972, a storm of protest from blue-collar workers greeted Senator McGovern's proposal for confiscatory estate taxes. They apparently wanted some big prizes maintained in the game. The silent majority did not want the yacht clubs closed forever to their children and grandchildren while those who had already become members kept sailing along.

On the other hand, those who reject the rules of the game on ethical grounds seem most offended by the reliance on "greed" as a key motivating force in economic life. Greed is deplored because it is an expression purely of self-interest, and because it aims at the acquisition of material things.

With proper awe for the fundamental philosophical issues concerning the virtues and practicalities of altruism as opposed to self-interest, I will still venture a few personal views. I do not find a reliance on self-interest offensive as an organizing principle

23. For a discussion of the mental attitude of the unemployed during the thirties, see E. Wight Bakke, *Citizens Without Work* (Yale University Press, 1940), especially pp. 201–02. For a current treatment of the aspirations of the poor, see Leonard Goodwin, *Do the Poor Want to Work?* (Brookings Institution, 1972), p. 112.

for the economy. First, selfishness is a safeguard against the much greater danger of blind allegiance to a leader or to the state. Second, self-interest is consistent with an enlightened selfishness that creates loyalties to family, community, and country, as institutions that benefit the individual and extend his range of interests. Third, I read the lesson of history as teaching that efforts to suppress the tendencies toward self-interest by the individual—in societies as noble as monasteries or as base as Fascist dictatorships—have also severely restricted the rights of the individual.

Nor am I offended by a competition that seeks prizes in the form of material possessions. Surely, some kinds of alternative rewards would be far more oppressive and more invidious—like feudal privileges and membership in the elite party. Indeed, if the losers can still lead a decent life, prizes for the winners in the form of swimming pools and bigger houses seem especially innocuous in terms of their social impact. In short, while I do not find reward for contribution ethically appealing, neither do I find it ethically intolerable—within pragmatic limits.

THE RECORD OF EFFICIENCY

The case for the efficiency of capitalism rests on the theory of the "invisible hand," which Adam Smith first set forth two centuries ago. Through the market, greed is harnessed to serve social purposes in an impersonal and seemingly automatic way. A competitive market transmits signals to producers that reflect the values of consumers. If the manufacture and distribution of a new product is profitable, the benefits it provides to buyers necessarily exceed the costs of production. And these costs in turn measure the value of the other outputs that are sacrificed by using labor and capital to make the new product. Thus, profitability channels resources into more productive uses and pulls them away from less productive ones. The producer has the incentive to make what consumers want and to make it in the least costly way. Nobody is asked to evaluate what is good for the system or for the society; if he merely pursues his own economic self-interest, he will automatically serve the social welfare.

While every market economy has fallen far short of the competitive ideal, the market has proved to be an efficient organizer of production in practice as well as in theory. The long-term record of U.S. economic growth and progress has confirmed many of the properties of market models.

The American economic system has at times developed knocks and required overhauls. The most serious knocks appeared in the Great Depression of the thirties; idle men and machines constituted an enormous inefficiency that any centrally planned system would have cured with massive doses of public investment. Many of those who view capitalism as a rotten system blame John Maynard Keynes and Franklin Delano Roosevelt for saving it; but those who view it as a magnificent system rarely credit them with saving it.

With the basically Keynesian policies of the postwar generation, the social costs of overall imbalances—the burden of inflation as well as unemployment—have been held to a small fraction of those of the Great Depression. Growth and material progress have been remarkable. Of course, the engine still has its knocks. The system remains blemished by monopoly. For too long, it ignored the social costs of production processes that blighted the natural environment. It has not crowned the consumer after two centuries of proclaiming his sovereignty. It still has not stabilized the value of money or reliably provided adequate job opportunities. And I could go on and on spelling out its defects. Still, in comparison with any other production system in man's history, or any blueprint currently on any drawing board, the American economy must get a high performance rating. Judging it as a system of production, I see no case for trading it in for a new model.

Any case for a trade-in rests squarely on the tradeoff: the efficiency is bought at the cost of inequalities in income and wealth and in the social status and power that go along with income and wealth. These inequalities stem from the private ownership of property, including the basic means of production, and from market-determined wages and salaries. The disparities need not be so large as they are today, and they can be trimmed by a variety of approaches that I will discuss in chapters 3 and 4. But those approaches, which leave the capitalist system basically intact, also leave the highest and lowest incomes far apart.

THE COLLECTIVIZED ECONOMY

A much more massive and more rapid equalization of income would probably require a new economic system as an alternative to capitalism. The chief rival to capitalism and the one that promises greater equality is, of course, socialism. Its key characteristic is that the state (rather than individuals) is the chief owner of income-producing property and hence the principal employer of labor. Every economy is a blend of private and public property, and the dividing line between socialism and capitalism is blurred. In the view of some, America went socialist once the national parks were created. To others, the systems of Western European countries whose ruling parties call themselves socialist—as in the United Kingdom and Scandinavia—are timid imitations of genuine socialism. In the United States, the currently relevant political issues focus on modest changes in the scope of public services and public ownership, rather than wholesale reforms of the institutional structure. Yet, to understand the nature of the system better, it is helpful to consider the implications of a drastic shift from the mixed capitalism of today to a thoroughgoing socialist system. How might equality and efficiency be affected in a collectivized American economy?

Compensation or Confiscation?

In the first place, socialism can provide a rapid and substantial redistribution of income only if nationalization is carried out by paying property owners much less than the market value of their assets.

As one of its initial tasks, a new socialist order would have to fix the compensation for the former owners of nationalized property. If it generously paid the owners fully and fairly appraised market values, the resulting redistribution of income would be shockingly small. Using 1973 data illustratively, I shall work through the arithmetic of a very ambitious socialist program that nationalized the entire corporate sector, at the same time providing full compensation. The state would then receive total corporate profits, amounting to $123 billion a year. But since it was previously collecting $50 billion out of that total from corporate income taxes and approximately another $8 billion from personal income taxes on dividends and capital gains on corporate equities, the net addition to government revenues would be $65 billion a year (123 − 50 − 8). On the other side, the state would pay the owners, at market value, a little more than $1 trillion, for which it would have to issue bonds. At an optimistic 7 percent interest rate on those bonds, Uncle Sam's annual interest bill would be raised by $72 billion. But offsetting that, in part, would be about $20 billion received back in taxes, leaving $52 billion as the after-tax cost. The resulting net transfer of after-tax income away from property owners is thus about $13 billion (65 − 52)—or just 1 percent of GNP.[24] "Fair" expropriation has less potential than tax reform.

24. Most of these figures are drawn from the official national income accounts. After consulting with Joseph Pechman, I pegged the marginal tax rate on dividends and interest at 27 percent, allowing for nontaxable recipients. The price-earnings ratio is assumed to be 14.2, Standard and Poor's average for 1973, yielding a value of $1,035 billion.

The general point here has long been recognized. See, for example, A. C. Pigou, *Socialism versus Capitalism* (Macmillan, 1937), p. 25: ". . . the official advocates of socialism, at least in this country, . . . propose to purchase the means of production from their present holders at a fair valuation. . . . the interest . . . will be roughly equivalent to what the private holders are now receiving as income from their property." However, some advocates of socialism argue that, once the state takes over and collectivizes investment decisions, income and wealth taxes on the rich can be made far stiffer without fear of the inefficiencies of adverse incentive effects. (See ibid., pp. 28–29.) I find that case for socialism as a prerequisite for tax reform strained and unconvincing.

With compensation at full market value, that kitty could not be appreciably enlarged by even broader socialization, which included noncorporate businesses, the real estate of individual landlords, and farm land and equipment. Socialism could really dent the distribution of income right from the start only if it paid owners much less than the value of their assets or, in the extreme, confiscated with no compensation at all. At that extreme, the stakes do get big: with no compensation, the elimination of all private property income from corporate and noncorporate businesses and real estate could bring $100 billion a year into the federal treasury; and if all interest were banned, including that on savings accounts and insurance, the figure would easily exceed $150 billion. That would be a revolution—and a bloody one. It would annihilate the constitutional rights of the affluent, and would clobber the welfare of small savers as well as universities, philanthropic organizations, and the beneficiaries of pension funds.

The Socialist Labor Market

Even more important, it is doubtful that labor incomes would be significantly equalized, unless the free choice of jobs were eliminated. Obviously, the chief managers of state enterprises would not have to be paid the huge salaries that now go to the top executives of giant corporations. But that would be a tiny benefit; if the maximum annual salary were set at $60,000 (the present pay of a U.S. Cabinet member), the total amount saved would be only a fraction of one percent of the national wage bill.

Beyond that, the redistribution would depend on the operation of the labor market. To level off high salaries, the new American socialist order might follow the precedents of older socialist countries, establishing itself as the sole employer of professional and managerial workers, and preventing state enterprises from competing actively with one another for their services. The supply of such workers would not be seriously impaired. Even modest differentials in income should suffice to attract youths into accounting and engineering, particularly if the state financed their education. But the demand would explode. If the wages of engineers were only trivially higher than those of assembly-line workers, any manager properly trained to cut costs by the Harvard State-Enterprise School would want to hire more engineers.

The government might try to use two sets of books to allocate the inadequate supply of professional workers among the demanders. It would then charge against the budget of the plant manager the efficiency wages (marginal product) of professional workers while setting a much lower scale of pay checks to be actually handed to those workers. What a mess that would be! For example, an engineer would have little incentive to pull up stakes in order to take a more productive job in another plant if it offered no significant pay hike.

As a more likely way out, the top planners might set for managers a quota of highly skilled workers as a proportion of their total work force—say, 5 percent of the employees of an electronics factory could be engineers. But then the state would have to provide the supplies to fill these quotas. Somewhere down that road, the freedom of individuals to make occupational and job choices would surely get lost, as it is in fact in many collectivized economies.[25] Qualified employees would essentially be drafted into jobs that needed to be filled. Of course, the loss of the right to quit might be compensated by the gain of a right not to be fired. Tenure is likely to be more common in a socialist system than under private enterprise, just as it is most prevalent in the nonprofit and public sectors of the U.S. economy. Still, by the values of most Americans, that exchange would not be a good trade.

As another alternative, the top planners might empower managers to compete freely for workers, with wages determined by that competition and with the workers getting the wages that are bid. That becomes merely a transplant of the capitalist labor market,

25. To be sure, the freedom of occupational choice under American capitalism is far from unlimited. The student who is not admitted to law school (or who is unable to pay the tuition) cannot become a lawyer. But even so the menu of choices is a long one.

and it should not be expected to generate a significant increase in the equality of labor incomes.[26] Progressive taxation keeps looking better and better.

Productive Efficiency

Centrally planned socialist countries have demonstrated that they can generate brisk growth of real GNP. But those results are subject to an efficiency discount on two different grounds. First, inefficiencies that do not hold down the measured real GNP arise from difficulties of instructing and scoring plant managers in the absence of a price system. As one classical example points out, if the performance of a nail factory is judged by the number of nails it produces, then the manager will strive to make lots of tiny nails; if it is scored by the weight of its output, then production will shift toward huge nails.[27] Second and more significantly, the outputs of the system follow the preferences of planners rather than the preferences of customers. Even the most consumer-oriented central planner cannot respond to the consumer's will as reliably as a profit-oriented capitalist executive must respond in a competitive environment.[28]

26. Professional economists will recognize this as a controversial issue. For example, Lester Thurow develops evidence that labor is currently paid less than its marginal product. I suspect that his procedure for correcting for cyclical underutilization tends to understate the marginal product of capital. See Lester C. Thurow, "Disequilibrium and the Marginal Productivity of Capital and Labor," *Review of Economics and Statistics,* Vol. 50 (February 1968), pp. 23–31.

27. Charles L. Schultze, "The Role of Incentives, Penalties, and Rewards in Attaining Effective Policy," in *The Analysis and Evaluation of Public Expenditures: The PPB System,* A Compendium of Papers Submitted to the Subcommittee on Economy in Government of the Joint Economic Committee, 91 Cong. 1 sess. (1969), pp. 221–22. See also Assar Lindbeck, *The Political Economy of the New Left: An Outsider's View* (Harper & Row, 1971), p. 40.

28. Henry Wallich essentially accepts the standard of planners' preferences in reaching the heterodox conclusion (for a conservative!) that socialism is inherently as efficient as capitalism. His case for capitalism then rests solely on the preservation of freedom. Implicit throughout his book is the assumption that an American socialist regime would sacrifice freedom whenever it conflicted with efficiency. He concedes, however, that British socialism has not followed such a practice. See Henry C. Wallich, *The Cost of Freedom* (Harper, 1960).

Back in the thirties, several economists designed interesting models to demonstrate that efficient allocation, consumer sovereignty, and free worker choice could be attained in a collectivized economy.[29] In these models of market-oriented socialism, the managers are given an operational set of instructions to do what managers of private enterprise should be doing in a competitive economy. That blueprint for decentralized socialism relied on markets and prices at least as heavily as does our current economy.

Despite its initial appeal, the blueprint gathers dust on the drawing board; it has never been seriously applied in building an actual socialist economy, and the intellectual debate over market socialism has itself died with a whimper.[30] Even theoretically, the system could not solve most of the problems that baffle a capitalist economy—like inequalities of labor income. Some old problems showed up in new forms. For example, no sure cure for monopoly emerged since the state managers had incentives to improve their performance rating (the equivalent of increasing their profits) by exploiting their substantial monopoly power. The top economic officials of the government would then have to assume the antitrust role of a capitalist economy to ensure that the managers really played the game as though they were perfect competitors. Nor did market socialism offer a breakthrough for most of the key problems of interdependence in industrial society, such as pollution. If managers are told to minimize costs, and pollution is not charged as a cost, socialist smoke will obscure the sun as surely as does capitalist smoke. And if fees or regulations can make socialist managers respect the environment, the same rules can be imposed by government on private enterprises.

29. Most notable is the work of Oskar Lange, "On the Economic Theory of Socialism," in Benjamin E. Lippincott (ed.), *On the Economic Theory of Socialism* (University of Minnesota Press, 1938).

30. For the definitive obituary, see Abram Bergson, "Market Socialism Revisited," *Journal of Political Economy*, Vol. 75 (October 1967), pp. 655–73.

A government-owned and government-operated economy would undoubtedly alter drastically the system now employed in our mixed economy for the production and distribution of knowledge. The basic problem of efficient allocation in this area is that the search for, and development of, knowledge and information can be exceedingly costly, while the distribution and dissemination are typically very inexpensive. Indeed, unless special legal provisions make it feasible, the protection of private property rights in knowledge and information is inherently difficult; in the absence of laws establishing patents, copyrights, and authorizations for industrial secrecy, there would be little scope for profit by inventors, authors, and idea producers. And hence there would be little market incentive to invest in the production of knowledge.

The present system operates on a set of compromises. In certain kinds of basic research, the fruits of the knowledge are deemed to be exceedingly important for general dissemination; these areas are largely financed by either the public or nonprofit sectors, and the findings are made available essentially to everyone. For the development of other types of knowledge, market incentives are provided by creating property rights and hence profitability for the successful producer. That gives the producer some monopoly power over his brain children and allows him to price them in a way that is clearly inefficient. Whenever the introduction of a new drug or a new electrical appliance is slowed down or made less pervasive as a result of its patent royalty, society is tolerating an inefficiency. Similar inefficiencies emerge whenever movies and books are produced in sequence of first-run or hardback and second-run or paperback, and whenever a concert, lecture, or sports event is priced to leave empty seats. In all of those widespread instances, something that has little cost to the producer and could have substantial value to the consumer is being rationed restrictively.

The present system is neither efficient nor esthetic, and yet I find it difficult to visualize a fundamental revision that would be a clear improvement. In particular, I do not find a collectivized solution appealing. The socialist blueprint seems most promising in its ability to curb the wastes of advertising and the distortions of market information that the consumer now endures. And yet even here the ultimate advantage seems slight. The difficulties of regulating the quantity, the quality, and the accuracy of advertising reflect the enormous problems and dangers of censorship. Everyone "knows" beyond a reasonable doubt that beer advertising is a sheer waste, while newspaper ads by supermarkets and drug stores provide useful information. But I would not want the government making rules based on such "known facts," which cannot be tested against objective criteria. I certainly would not entrust to the planners decisions on how much foreign companies, like Volkswagen, Wilkinson, and Sony, could spend on ads that compete with state enterprises. I do not see sound criteria for even the most noble planning board to determine how much and what kind of product information should be distributed or how the dishonest or overly enthusiastic manager might be kept in check. The problems the government now faces in trying to regulate the activity efficiently would continue to plague it if it were operating the activity.[31]

In handling big and small decisions on consumer product choice and innovations, I would expect an American brand of socialism—like the actual brands elsewhere—to be far inferior to the mixed capitalist economy. Socialism would provide no mechanism for an Edwin Land of Polaroid to buck a nationalized Eastman Kodak. It would offer neither strong incentives nor outlets for that unsung pathbreaker for women's rights—the inventor of permanent-press sheets and shirts. Under socialism, who would decide to finance the development of xerography or microfilm? Who would turn grocery stores into supermarkets? And above all, who would open a discount house? No matter how hard I strain, I cannot visualize a nationalized discount house or a private one being allowed to

---

31. See the discussion of advertising and related issues in Lindbeck, *Political Economy of the New Left*, pp. 40–49.

compete vigorously with state retail enterprises. The absence of discount houses can serve as the defining criterion of a collectivized economy. To be sure, I can think of counter-examples. The American consumer might have been offered a selection of small cars sooner if the country had a nationalized automobile industry (as well as if it had a more competitive private industry). On balance, I would expect an American version of socialism to be far less flexible, less innovative, and less experimental than the mixed present system.

One of the great merits of the existing system is the way it fosters experimentation by letting people play with their own money or with shareholders' money that is voluntarily put at risk. Although rigid bureaucracies often develop in our giant private corporations, far more bureaucratization of economic life would have to be expected under nonmarket socialism. In particular, in that system, all money would be taxpayers' money and would have to be treated with the same respect, caution, and rigidity that are currently evident in the public sector.

Costs of Bureaucracy

Because the government gets its funds from taxpayers by mandatory, and not voluntary, decisions, there is no room for the principle of caveat emptor in the area of public services. The government must be accountable to the citizens, and accountability is as costly in resources as it is precious to the integrity of the political process. Bureaucratic red tape is neither an accident nor a reflection of bad rules or inept officials: it is the result of the obligation of political decisionmakers to be cautious, to avoid capriciousness, to take account of the full range of interests and impacts of the course they adopt, and to guard against any misuse of taxpayers' money. Public officials follow the Ten Commandments of their profession, which proclaim that thou shalt not be experimental or venturesome or flexible. Those safeguards on accountability are necessary. The Civil Service Commission should have tougher rules about firing people than any private employer. The Office of Management and Budget should spend $20 to prevent the theft of $1 of public funds. Senators should have to defend their pay to their constituents. The Appropriations Committees of the Congress should ponder expenditures that could be approved swiftly by a vice president in a business corporation.

Another commandment proclaims that once something is given, it shall not be taken away. A congressman has to defend to his constituents any loss of government jobs in the district, and will be blamed for such losses far more than if a private firm moves out. As a result, defense bases and veterans' hospitals stay open for decades after they have become inefficient and obsolete. Protections for owners of small farms and businesses and for construction workers that may have made sense in the thirties remain nonsensically on the statute books today. And those irreversibilities can come from good legislators responsive to their constituents, not just evil men tainted by money. Any socialist model—other than the dusty market blueprint—entrusts more power to the administrative systems of government and proliferates these bureaucratic costs.

CONCLUSION

I have argued in this chapter that the issue of government versus private ownership of industry has little to do with freedom, but much to do with efficiency. Any realistic version of American socialism that I can visualize would not encroach dangerously on the rights that are precious to me. But precisely because it would operate within the constraints of preserving these rights, the collectivized system would, in my judgment, achieve only a small improvement in equality at the expense of a significant worsening of efficiency. I regard it as vital that private enterprise continue to be the main mechanism for organizing economic activity in those areas where experimentation and innovation are important, and in those where flexibility matters more than accountability. And those areas represent a large part of the economy. In expressing this judgment, I am not allying myself with those who would shout down every proposal to expand the scope of public services or public ownership as another step to socialism (and hence an obvious misstep). Americans should be pleased, in retrospect, that the government got into the business of pensions and unemployment insurance, of financing basic research, and of electric power.

As in the case of public power, a limited government role in a predominantly private industry can generate benefits that flow in both directions. The public company is constrained and tested by the record of the private companies, while the private ones are obliged to measure up to the yardstick established by the public activity. On these grounds, I am sympathetic to various analogous recent proposals for petroleum and coal.

More generally, I believe that the government does some things efficiently. It is my impression that check-writing and check-collecting agencies like the Social Security Administration and the Internal Revenue Service are paragons of efficiency. The National Institutes of Health and the National Science Foundation seem to handle with skill some delicate problems in promoting the production of knowledge. In addition to the things the government can do well, there are functions the government must perform in filling the gaps left by the marketplace and in regulating private activities. Precisely because the federal government must take on so many tasks, I would prefer to keep it out of the doubtful areas in order to focus its energy and effort on the essential ones, and to safeguard against excessive growth of the bureaucracy. If I were drawing blueprints for a new economy, I would have no conviction about whether airlines, for example, should be publicly or privately owned. But, given history, crusading for nationalization (rather than regulatory reform) in that area makes no sense to me. I see hundreds of more promising crusades, most of which do not add to the power of, or burdens on, the federal bureaucracy.

My views on the capacities and limitations of the federal bureaucracy reflect my experience of five years in the executive branch of the government, and my first-hand encounters with the difficult tradeoff between accountability and flexibility. Perhaps if I had spent five years in the management of a giant corporation, I would have a clearer appreciation of its limitations and a somewhat different view of the balance.

In general, perhaps I have been attacking straw blueprints in explaining why both Soviet-type socialism and market-model socialism seem to me to be unsatisfactory alternatives to the mixed capitalist system of contemporary America. If there are better blueprints for an American collectivized economy, I would like to see them and their specific proposals for organizing economic activity. I even hope that my strictures will encourage some of the radical reformers to unroll their blueprints. Those who rally behind the slogan of "power to the people" have an obligation to explain how that power would be organized (and properly limited) and how it would deal with the nagging tradeoff of equality and efficiency. In particular, they must face up to the choice between the market and bureaucracy (or else offer a brand-new third alternative). As Lindbeck put it, "It may be possible to make a strong case against either markets or administrative systems, but if we are against both [as most radicals are] we are in trouble."[32]

There may well be reasonable alternatives to the present system that would be more egalitarian without becoming less efficient. Conceivably, the Israeli-type kibbutz could come to America with a decentralized system of public ownership in which communities operated industrial enterprises. I find it challenging to imagine the nuts and bolts in such a system—how property income would be distributed; how the labor market would be organized; and how funds would be raised for capital investment.

32. Lindbeck, *Political Economy of the New Left*, p. 32.

I find it easier to imagine the development of an American economic system in which large enterprises would be owned and managed by workers. Yugoslavian socialism is said to have important elements of such worker control, and some traces of it (like faculty power in universities) appear in the nonprofit sector of our economy. Voluntary agreements and arrangements in the United States may move in that direction over the decades ahead. In some respects, it is puzzling that so little worker control has developed to date. In principle, profit sharing and participatory decisionmaking by workers could strengthen the loyalties and the incentives of employees in a firm. In general, however, American business and labor are not choosing this route; they seem to relish their adversary roles and look for viable ways of conflicting rather than new means of joining forces. Like a pair of old tomcats, they seem to enjoy their habitual scraps. In a sense, American workers thus far have displayed a preference for consolidating their positions as consumers rather than establishing a beachhead as capitalists. Opportunities for better compensation are captured in the form of higher wages to buy homes and dishwashers, and retirement benefits to raise living standards in old age, rather than in the common stock of the employing firm. But these attitudes may change in an evolutionary way.

Indeed, the most confident prediction I can make about the American economic system is that it will evolve and adapt if its basic framework is preserved and strengthened rather than scrapped. The capacity to adapt gradually is the greatest virtue of our present mixed system. Reforming it and promoting its evolution are feasible objectives, and are far more attractive to me than scrapping it. The alternatives I can see threaten efficiency, and they promise a limited increase in equality only at the expense of dangerous and costly bureaucratization. Although the ethical case for capitalism is totally unpersuasive, the efficiency case is thoroughly compelling to me.

CHAPTER THREE

EQUALITY OF INCOME AND OPPORTUNITY

The concept of economic equality is hard to define or to measure. It might be impossible to recognize complete equality if it existed; but inequality is very easy to recognize. A short trip from the dreary slums to the classy areas of the suburbs is an interplanetary voyage measured in economic differentials. But it takes the traveler through a lot of territory occupied by the middle class, whose economic status is neither dreary nor classy.

As a foundation for the discussion of policy measures to narrow differentials, I shall describe in general terms (with only a handful of facts and figures) the existing magnitude and character of inequality in the distribution of material welfare. I shall then discuss some of the underlying causes of inequality and the roles of choice and chance in creating high and low incomes. That discussion will raise issues about the relationship between equality of income and equality of opportunity; in the second half of the chapter, I will focus on inequalities of opportunity and their consequences for both efficiency and equality of income.

THE DISTRIBUTION OF ECONOMIC WELFARE

Income and wealth are the two box-score numbers in the record book on people's economic positions. Income is the more important of the two, because it provides the basic purchasing power for maintaining a standard of living; moreover, when property incomes are included, the income distribution reflects holdings of wealth.

Nonetheless, wealth is important in its own right and deserves some attention. In part, people accumulate wealth by saving the extra margin of income above their consumption expenditures. Over a wide range of income that spans the middle of the distribution, families save a roughly constant small fraction of their incomes. But at the very bottom of the income pyramid, people accumulate debts—to the extent they can borrow—rather than wealth. And at the very top, people save substantial fractions of their incomes, accumulating the bulk of the nation's private wealth. In addition to saving, receipts of gifts and bequests are an important source of large wealth. Much of the net worth of the wealthy reflects marketable assets, such as securities and real estate, which are passed on by inheritance from one generation to the next. In contrast, middle-class wealth typically takes the form of furniture, household equipment, and automobiles, which are worn out over the years rather than bequeathed to heirs. Middle-income families typically own their homes; indeed, roughly two-thirds of American families do. For most, that structure is the largest entry on their balance sheet, and the most important asset that is sold or bequeathed.

The differences in saving patterns and in bequest patterns of rich and poor make the distribution of wealth far more unequal than that of income.[1] The richest 1 percent of American families have about one-third of the wealth, while they receive about 6 percent of after-tax income. The bottom half of all families hold only 5 percent of total wealth, although they receive roughly a quarter of all income.[2]

1. An analytical model of inequality of wealth is developed in J. E. Meade, *Efficiency, Equality and the Ownership of Property* (Harvard University Press, 1965), pp. 42–46, 82–87.

2. The wealth estimates are taken from Dorothy S. Projector, "Survey of Financial Characteristics of Consumers," *Federal Reserve Bulletin*, Vol. 50 (March 1964),

Income Inequality

Since dividends, interest, rent, and other property incomes come from wealth holdings, those types of income reflect the concentration of wealth and flow mainly to the top income groups. Including self-employment income from unincorporated businesses and farms and from professional practices, property income accounts for about one-fifth of total family income in the nation. One-tenth of all income comprises "transfer payments," items like social security and unemployment benefits for which no current services are provided in return. Transfers are the big equalizer, flowing principally to families whose earned incomes are low. By one statistical measure of income inequality, the degree of inequality of family incomes in 1970 would have been more than double its actual size in the absence of any government transfers.[3]

The vast bulk—about two-thirds—of the income of American households comes from wages and salaries. Their distribution lies between the extreme lopsidedness of property incomes and the equalizing tendencies of transfers. Except among the lowest tenth of all families in the income distribution (where transfers are dominant) and among the top 3 or 4 percent (where property income prevails), wages and salaries account for at least half of the incomes of all groups.

For all families (excluding unrelated individuals), average income net of income taxes ("disposable" income, which is the

---

p. 291. Unless otherwise referenced, the income distribution data cited throughout chapters 3 and 4 rely on Daniel B. Radner and John C. Hinrichs, "Size Distribution of Income in 1964, 1970, and 1971," *Survey of Current Business*, Vol. 54 (October 1974), pp. 19–31. Their concept includes various types of nonmoney income and adjusts for the underreporting of both transfers and property income in the Census surveys. I take the liberty of guessing where 1974 would stand and how disposable personal income (rather than their personal income measure) would emerge.

3. See *The Annual Report of the Council of Economic Advisers, February 1974*, Table 49, p. 178. The measure of inequality used is the variance of the natural logarithm of income. For a criticism of this statistical measure, see Edward C. Budd, in *The 1974 Economic Report of the President*, Hearings before the Joint Economic Committee, 93 Cong. 2 sess. (1974), Pt. 1, pp. 140–41.

concept I shall stress) was about $14,000 in 1974. Because some people receive ten and even a hundred times the average, the distribution is not symmetrical or bell-shaped like that of height or of scores on most ability tests. The family that stood exactly in the middle of the income pyramid—the median family that has half the population above it and half below—had an after-tax income of about $12,000. That median is less than the average because of the lopsidedness of the distribution. At the very bottom, 11 percent of the population are in families with incomes below the poverty line, which was drawn, sensibly but hardly scientifically, as the purchasing power required to buy a specified market basket of minimum adequacy. For a nonfarm family of four, that budget would have cost about $5,000 in 1974. The bottom fifth of all families had after-tax incomes under $7,000, and thus do not get much above the poverty line. The bottom third extended to about $9,500.

At the high end, the top fifth of families had incomes above $18,000. At a disposable income of about $28,000, a family got into the top 5 percent of the income pyramid. Most people at that level consider themselves middle-income rather than upper-income and are shocked to learn that their incomes exceed those of nineteen out of twenty American families. But it is only by comparison with their own friends, neighbors, and coworkers that they are just average. Or, in another sense, they do not have enough contact with average Americans to realize how unusual their economic status is.

The income distribution can be made to look soothingly equal or shockingly unequal, depending on how the figures are lined up. On the one hand, the portion of the income of the very affluent in excess of $50,000 per household amounts to only about 2 percent of total disposable income. That seems reassuring. On the other hand, the top 1 percent of families (those with roughly $50,000 and above) have as much after-tax income as nearly all the families in the bottom 20 percent. That seems terrible to me. And I find it disturbing that the top fifth of families have about as much after-tax income as the bottom three-fifths.

The relative distribution of family income has changed very little in the past generation. The nation took one big step toward equality during World War II; throughout the postwar period, the top income groups have received a substantially smaller share of total income than they had in the prosperous years of the twenties.[4] Since the late forties, however, the proportion of income absorbed by each fifth of the population has inched only a tiny bit further toward equality. Roughly, at all points on the income scale, family disposable incomes in real terms (that is, corrected for inflation) have doubled in the last generation. As a result of the rising tide of progress, any average or absolute measure of real family income records dramatic improvement. The poverty-line living standard that was out of the reach of 11 percent of Americans in 1973 would have exceeded the incomes of about one-third a generation ago. But the percentage gaps between rich and poor have remained essentially constant, of course implying that the dollar differences between them have widened. And relative incomes have cultural and sociological importance. No self-respecting family in Boston can sleep in the streets, although that practice is quite acceptable in Bombay. Less dramatically, incomes that would have been regarded as reasonable and respectable a generation ago now leave a family outside the mainstream of middle-class life. The inability to own homes or cars or take vacations represents a greater deprivation to people who see most of their fellow citizens enjoying them.

Thus, while both the rich and the poor have experienced rising living standards, poverty remains the plight of a substantial group of Americans, and the large relative disparities in the income distribution continue to mar the social scene.

4. Simon Kuznets, *Shares of Upper Income Groups in Income and Savings* (National Bureau of Economic Research, 1953), pp. 32–40.

Family Income and "True" Equality

The box-score numbers on family incomes cannot tell the whole story of the distribution of economic welfare among American families. First, families differ in their consumption needs and consequently may require different levels of income in order to achieve the same economic welfare. Second, families can finance their living standards not only out of their incomes of the current year, but also by dipping into their wealth or borrowing against their prospective incomes. Third, some people earn higher incomes by sacrificing aspects of their economic welfare in ways that do not show up in the income distribution. Fourth, others obtain some rewards that are not counted in money income and hence are not reflected in the quantitative distributions.

NEEDS. It obviously takes a larger consumption budget for a large family to achieve the same standard of living as a small one. Parents in big families may not sacrifice their welfare if they consciously choose to have lots of kids because they get more fun from children than from vacations or cars; but the children of big families unambiguously attain a lower level of economic welfare than those in small ones with the same incomes. Whether or not they enjoy siblings, the kids rarely get a vote on family size. When economists correct for differences in family size in their studies (for example, in estimating the number of people below the poverty line), they find that a certain amount of economic deprivation comes from unusually high needs rather than especially low incomes. Occasionally, unusual needs arise from special medical or educational requirements of some family members. In these cases, the income distribution hides some dimensions of inequality.

On the other hand, some differences in needs are related to differences in income opportunities. The cost of living is higher in cities than in rural communities, but so is the opportunity to earn income. In this sense, income differentials between urban and rural Americans may overstate differences in their economic welfare.

SUPPLEMENTARY SOURCES. Some families can maintain standards of living that are high relative to their annual incomes because they can finance some expenditures by dipping into wealth, or by borrowing. For example, those retired people who have a comfortable nest egg are better off than their incomes (including both property and pension receipts) would suggest. Similarly, some people with particularly large fluctuations in income from one year to the next can nonetheless maintain a fairly steady living standard over time by saving in the good years and dissaving in the bad ones; thus they experience less deprivation (and less affluence) than their annual incomes imply.

VOLUNTARY NONMONETARY SACRIFICES. Some families earn higher incomes than others because their members work more by moonlighting or seizing opportunities for overtime, or because a larger number of family members work. A hard-working family may achieve its extra income by sacrificing leisure that other families with the same opportunities regard as indispensable. Suppose the Smiths and the Stones each have two school-age children and the husbands have the same kind of job with the same income, but Mrs. Stone chooses to be a full-time homemaker while Mrs. Smith works part-time. The Smith family income will run substantially above that of the Stones, but presumably the Stones do not wish to give up the time that Mrs. Stone spends at home, perhaps caring for her children, or cooking and housecleaning, or just enjoying her leisure. To the extent that both families have the same opportunities, their economic welfare cannot be significantly different, even though their capacity to buy consumer goods and services will be different.

Some families earn larger incomes by accepting jobs that are inherently unpleasant, exhausting, or risky, but offer extra pay to workers to compensate for the poor working conditions. Extra earnings that reflect a premium for being a steeplejack or an embalmer or working on the night shift do not constitute a fundamental inequality in economic welfare.

NONMONETARY BONUSES. In actual practice, the income pre-miums that are equalizing—compensating for the lower attractive-ness of a job—are swamped by income differentials that accentuate such nonmonetary differentials as social status and recognition. Public attitudes about good jobs reflect many considerations, of which the inherent nature of the work experience is one small part. A surgeon and a butcher operate with similar tools in com-parably bloody environments; but the two occupations are poles apart in status, and the income differentials accentuate rather than neutralize the nonmonetary benefits. In general, the same jobs that draw high incomes also evoke social applause and high status. To be sure, the correlation is not perfect. Coupon clippers and executives of big corporations do not get status commensurate with their income, while clergymen, top public officials, and even some teachers are more richly rewarded with social approval than with money income. While the equalizing differential presents a tradeoff to the worker between money income and the nonpecuni-ary features of a job, the accentuating differential forces some into a tie-in sale of low income and low status.

These various qualifications of the distribution of family incomes are interesting for several reasons. They provide some searching tests and criteria of the real meaning of economic equality. They also reveal how difficult it would be to derive a precise measure of economic inequality. If complete equality were seriously the goal, solving all these conceptual problems and making all the proper corrections and allowances would be cru-cial. Moreover, the qualifications are useful reminders that some distributive problems of social consequence—like large families and special consumption needs—are buried in the distribution of family incomes. But they are also reminders of why some of the inequality in the measured distribution of income is not a seri-ous social problem, insofar as it reflects people's choices on how much to work, where to live, and whether to take advantage of equalizing differentials.

Cafeterias, Casinos, and the Income Distribution

Those who minimize the social significance of economic inequality emphasize the last category of qualifications—the income differentials that merely reflect different tastes and voluntary choices. These are the cases in which unequal incomes emerge despite equivalent options to earn income. But the labor market is not, in fact, a cafeteria line, and what people get on their trays bears only a slight relationship to their preferences. The tradeoffs of income against leisure, working conditions, and the like explain only a tiny portion of income inequality and probably even less of poverty.

A larger, but still limited, portion of inequality can be related to personal characteristics of individuals or families. If one had to estimate the income of a specified family, it would help to have information about the social and economic position of their parents, any inheritances received by members of the family, their educational attainments (and other endowments of "human capital"), their ages, and the geographical region and the size of the community in which the family lives. Incidentally, once the educational attainments of the working members are known, additional information on their IQ scores helps very little, if at all, to estimate their income.[5] Nonetheless, an estimate made with full knowledge of all these background and personal characteristics would still be subject to a very wide margin of error.

No quantifiable and measurable set of personal traits can pin down economic success or failure. Because of that, some frustrated observers tend to view the marketplace as a casino, featuring games of chance.[6] But that line of argument has two basic flaws. First, even if market prizes and penalties are like a lottery

5. Samuel Bowles and Valerie I. Nelson, "The 'Inheritance of IQ' and the Intergenerational Reproduction of Economic Inequality," *Review of Economics and Statistics,* Vol. 56 (February 1974), pp. 39–51.

6. The chance factor is stressed heavily by Christopher Jencks and others, *Inequality: A Reassessment of the Effect of Family and Schooling in America* (Basic Books, 1972); see, for example, pp. 8–9.

in lacking any systematic relation to the personal characteristics of the winners and losers, they may be serving essential functions as incentives to channel resources and hence promote economic efficiency. Although the invention of the electric light bulb was a random event to both the glass maker and the candlestick maker, the prizes and penalties levied on them by the market helped to pull resources into glass manufacturing and to push them out of candlestick making. What is random for the individual may be grand design for the system.

Second, the fact that behavioral scientists cannot adequately explain the verdicts of the marketplace may reveal more about the present state of behavioral science than about the functioning of the market. It is presumptuous in the extreme to conclude that anything one can't explain must be a lottery. By that reasoning, chess must be a game of chance, since no one can explain success in it. Similarly, the marketplace may be rewarding in an entirely systematic fashion some traits that are thus far unidentified or at least unquantified, such as looks, personality, shrewdness, single-mindedness, and talent for music, arts, athletics, and handiwork.

Much current research seeks to identify the extent and nature of the impact of family-related background factors on incomes. Clearly, there is some tendency for the affluence or poverty of the father to be visited upon the son. As Christopher Jencks and his associates report, the sons of families in the top fifth of the socioeconomic pyramid have average incomes 75 percent higher than those coming from the bottom fifth.[7] The authors of that study insist that the difference amounts to only 75 percent, stressing that the differential is a rather small fraction of the total variation among family incomes. But I would emphasize that it amounts to as much as 75 percent—by any reasonable standard an enormous differential.

Some of the causes of that differential are undoubtedly genetic or hereditary; substantial parts are environmental, including

7. Ibid., p. 213.

differences in the prenatal nutrition and medical care of rich and poor mothers, varying attitudes instilled in child rearing, and differential abilities to finance higher education. Obviously, society cannot repeal the hereditary factors, nor is it about to overturn the institution of familial child-rearing, which is highly valued by most Americans, including me. But some familial disadvantages can in principle be offset at a cost if society accepts Rawls' principle of redress. When kidney machines are subsidized, the principle of redress is accepted. Similar reasoning points to much broader applications. In fact, compensatory education for the children of disadvantaged families has been widely discussed and even attempted in some instances, apparently without much success. But that experience does not prove that compensatory measures can never succeed in any area at any time.

EQUALITY OF OPPORTUNITY

Much of the interest in the sources of inequality reflects a conviction that economic inequalities that stem from inequality of opportunity are more intolerable (and, at the same time, more remediable) than those that emerge even when opportunities are equal. But the concept of equality of opportunity is far more elusive than that of equality of income and it defies any meaningful measurement.[8] Basically it is rooted in the notion of a fair race, where people are even at the starting line in ways discussed in chapter 2. But, as I noted there, it is hard to find the starting line. Differences in natural abilities are generally accepted as relevant characteristics that are being tested in the race rather than as unfair headstarts and handicaps. At the other extreme, success that depends on whom you know rather than what you know is a clear case of inequality of opportunity. And it seems particularly unfair

8. An excellent discussion can be found in Kurt Klappholz, "Equality of Opportunity, Fairness and Efficiency," in Maurice Peston and Bernard Corry (eds.), *Essays in Honour of Lord Robbins* (International Arts and Sciences Press, 1972), pp. 247–56.

when the real issue is whom your father knows. The inheritance of natural abilities is on one side of the line of unequal opportunity, and the advantages of family position are clearly on the other. But much of the territory is unsettled. What aspects of the proverbial silver spoon should be regarded as creating inequality of opportunity? Does the line begin at differences in prenatal influences? Or at the benefits of better childhood health care, achievement-oriented training, educational attainment, family assistance in job placement, inheritance of physical property?

While the concept of equal opportunity has an indefinite boundary line, some areas of unequal opportunity are clearly evident. And some of these are amenable to remedial social action. The clearest cases are those outside the orbit of family relationships. Racial and sexual discrimination in jobs and pervasive preferential treatment in borrowing present obvious cases of inequality of economic opportunity. And they can be reduced by public policies that would enhance both equality of income and efficiency. In such cases, society can get more of two good things rather than sacrificing one for the other.

Discrimination in Job Opportunities

Whenever trading decisions in the marketplace are influenced by the personal characteristics of buyers and sellers as distinct from the quality and characteristics of the products they wish to deal in, that market generates an inequality of opportunity as well as an economic imperfection. Consider, for example, cases where job opportunities are influenced by race or sex. These may involve poorer pay for a given job—exploitation—or exclusion from good jobs. When a woman gets as good a job as a man with equal skills would obtain but is paid less, the exploitation creates unjustified inequalities; but it may not have much effect on efficiency, at least in the short run. On the other hand, if women are excluded from responsible jobs, they are prevented from using their skills to the fullest extent; that is inefficiency—in effect, the worker's hand is tied behind her back. The empirical evidence identifies exclusion as the main form of discrimination in labor markets. It produces a triplet of evils: unequal opportunity, unequal income, and inefficiency.

Moreover, unequal opportunity at one point in time generates unequal opportunity over time. Once people are excluded from good jobs, they are deprived of the incentives and opportunities to develop the skills that would otherwise qualify them for good jobs. A black will not invest in education for managerial positions if he has no hope of becoming a manager. If he is blocked from his firm's ladder-climbing career program, he accumulates fewer skills on the job. Thus, inefficiency can grow at compound interest.

Not everyone would agree with my interpretation of such unequal opportunity as an inefficiency. Consider the following argument. Employers have to take into account the tastes of their workers. Since people don't like to work in a plant or office with an 85 degree temperature, firms install air conditioning. That amenity is costly and it may not increase production, yet it may be an efficient way for employers to avoid losing workers. But now suppose that the employees of a firm get hot under the collar if they must accept women or blacks as coworkers in peer positions, or even hotter if they must take orders from female or black supervisors.[9] The employer must take those tastes into account too. If the least costly way is to refuse to hire women or blacks for good jobs, then how can that be inefficient? And, according to this argument, the market is merely transmitting signals of people's tastes and should not be blamed for bad tastes, any more than a TV set should be held responsible for poor programs.[10]

9. Obviously, it is peer association, and not mere propinquity, that offends discriminators. The widespread use of black servants, waiters, and so on, makes that clear. Social, not physical, distance is the issue.

10. The argument is a deliberate caricature, but its resemblance to Becker's analysis should be evident. See Gary S. Becker, *The Economics of Discrimination* (University of Chicago Press, 1957).

As I see it, that argument makes an important point. It explains why the political process rather than the marketplace must judge the legitimacy of some preferences. Society overrules the preferences of some would-be employers to hire people to beat up their enemies or to market adulterated products to consumers. When society opts for equal employment opportunity, it is overruling preferences for racial and sexual discrimination. It classifies those attitudes with the proclivity to hire thugs rather than with the propensity to shun heat.

In fact, the principle of equal employment opportunity was established as a right and removed from the sphere of the marketplace a decade ago. That action has been followed by a significant reduction of racial discrimination in labor markets. Black women have scored particularly impressive gains. The average earnings of black women aged 18 to 44 rose from about two-thirds those of their white counterparts in 1959, to more than 90 percent in 1969.[11] The size of the remaining gap is probably understated, because black women tend to work full-time and to stick with a working career continuously. But the substantial improvement must be genuine. The gain for black males is also significant, although it is much smaller and their position underlines the large remaining disadvantages. During the sixties, the earnings of black men in the age groups under 45 advanced from roughly 60 percent to roughly 70 percent of the corresponding white earnings.

I do not cite these figures as a cause for self-congratulation. (Indeed, the evidence of some backsliding in 1973 is a cause for self-examination.[12]) Nor do I view the attainment of equal employment opportunity (or any important right) as an accomplishment

11. Richard B. Freeman, "Changes in the Labor Market for Black Americans, 1948–72," *Brookings Papers on Economic Activity* (1:1973), especially table 3, p. 83.

12. U.S. Bureau of the Census, *Current Population Reports*, Series P-60, No. 97, "Money Income in 1973 of Families and Persons in the United States" (1975), pp. 6, 12.

to be measured in dollars. But I believe the record dramatizes the general point that political decisions about fair play can change economic behavior. It further illustrates the general possibility that what is good for equality may be good for efficiency. The narrowing of racial differentials during the sixties implied a gain of nearly one-fifth in the wages and salaries of blacks. That gain approached 1 percent of the nation's income.[13] When we can have more justice and more real GNP, society should make the most of it. It is economically important to capture the added growth that could be generated by a concerted and accelerated program of equalizing employment opportunity—as important in economic terms alone as it is, for example, to limit the drag on growth from higher costs of energy.

Discrimination in Access to Capital

Opportunities for greater efficiency and broader equality may be even more abundant in capital markets than in labor markets. By the impersonal criterion of the ideal market, everyone contemplating the same investment project should face exactly the same interest costs. That does not happen. In fact, the projects of the well-to-do typically get favored treatment. Wealthy investors often can tap their own funds rather than borrowing to finance their projects; when they do borrow, the lender can be more confident of repayment, regardless of how the project fares. Nobody lost money lending to Ford Motor Company for the ill-fated Edsel. Those were safe loans for a sick project.

The reverse side of this coin of favoritism for the wealthy is discrimination against the poor. The resulting inefficiency and inequality of opportunity curb investment by the poor in setting up businesses, in buying homes, in education, and in all forms of human capital. They pervade job decisions. For example, suppose

13. In calculating the economic gain to society, some discount for reduced exploitation (a small one, I think) is in order. The reduction in exclusion is fully a gain for the nation as well as for the disadvantaged.

a person can choose between two jobs: one offers $3.50 an hour initially with no chance for advancement; the second starts at $2.50 but could lead to a promotion to a $5-an-hour job after an apprenticeship period. Acting rationally, a person who cannot afford to wait will choose the former over the latter.

Low-income families face vastly higher effective interest rates than do average Americans; in some cases, when they simply cannot get access to funds, they are confronted by an infinite interest rate. Edward Banfield has rightly stressed the "present-orientedness" of the lower class.[14] But I believe that he wrongly views present-orientedness as a psychological mystery requiring some deep explanatory structure. As I see it, many of the poor act like there's no tomorrow because their main problem is surviving today. Saving and investment are hardly rational at the cost of survival. And the most important consequence is the inadequate development of the human resources of the children of poor families—which, I would judge, is one of the most serious inefficiencies of the American economy today.

Let me focus on one particular aspect of that inefficiency, its influence on the vast differences in rates of college attendance by income class. Among high school graduates with equal academic ability, the proportion going on to college averages nearly 25 percentage points lower for males (and nearly 35 for females) in the bottom socioeconomic quarter of the population than in the top quarter.[15] And that gap emerges from the same sources that make ownership of dishwashers vary enormously by income group.

14. Edward C. Banfield, *The Unheavenly City* (Little, Brown, 1970), pp. 210–37.
15. *Toward Equal Opportunity for Higher Education,* Report of the Panel on Financing Low-Income and Minority Students in Higher Education (College Entrance Examination Board, 1973), p. 12. The gap is widest in the next-to-the-bottom ability quarter, where enrollment rates for males range from 29 percent (bottom socioeconomic quarter) to 62 percent (top) and those for females from 25 percent to 66 percent. In the top ability quarter (where the differentials in attendance rates are smallest), the corresponding figures are 75 percent and 88 percent for males and 67 percent and 88 percent for females.

It reflects primarily the vastly different significance of the huge investment in college (including forgone earnings) for families at different income levels.

Given the amount of higher education now provided, the selection is clearly inefficient and excludes millions whose academic abilities exceed those of people who do attend.[16] A vigorous social effort to narrow the educational financing gap can improve both equality and efficiency. In a financing plan now experimentally used at Yale, the student is offered loans with an obligation to repay that is fixed not in dollars but rather as a fraction of his or her future income.[17] If the borrower's lifetime income turns out to be very high, the loan will be, in a sense, overpaid, but it will not prove burdensome; moreover, some of the good fortune can be attributed to the benefits of education. On the other hand, the person who does not earn much has no onerous commitment. For society, this concept could be incorporated in a voluntary social insurance plan that would operate in reverse sequence to the present old-age program. Young people get the money first and pay back later, with the repayment levied as a supplementary tax on income.

The Yale plan is an intriguing initiative designed to narrow the financing gap. I am not claiming that it is necessarily the best way to achieve the goal. Nor do I claim to know how much a program like this would help. But the direction is clear: equalizing financing opportunities for higher education is one of the ways by which the nation can obtain more efficiency and more equality—without sacrificing one for the other.

There are many possible remedies for the various inefficiencies associated with unequal opportunity. Some are being tried; many

16. My professional readers will realize why I state this point in terms of a redistribution of a *given* amount of higher education. The private benefit is then independent of the controversy on human capital vs. screening—a brawl I don't wish to join.

17. See the discussion (and citations) in Robert W. Hartman, "Equity Implications of State Tuition Policy and Student Loans," *Journal of Political Economy*, Vol. 80 (May/June 1972), Pt. 2, pp. S165–71.

are being seriously discussed. Government job-training programs are an attempt to compensate for the present-orientedness of the poor. Public clearinghouses for jobs attempt to overcome the high cost of obtaining information about employment. Some social scientists urge employers to rely more heavily on interviews and direct tests of relevant skills for jobs, rather than on diplomas, as screening devices in personnel recruitment. This is a constructive use of jawboning, encouraging private decisionmaking to promote equality of opportunity.

THE POTENTIAL OF EQUALIZED OPPORTUNITY

Nobody knows how much any combination of such measures could enhance equality of income or the efficiency of the economy. Guesses about their potential are in striking accord with general ideological positions; optimism hits a peak slightly left of center, and drops off in both directions. The right is convinced that opportunities are basically equal and that no heroic efforts at reform are needed. The left believes that no amount of equalization of education or hiring practices or the like will noticeably dent the amount of inequality. It views the system as rotten to the core rather than ragged at the edges. Of course, I want to believe that much of the inequality of income and wealth reflects inequalities of opportunity that can be efficiently corrected within the present institutional structure, just as conservatives want to believe that no corrections are necessary and radicals want to believe that no moderate corrections would be efficacious. All I would claim is that such efforts deserve a real try.

Opportunity and Results

I am confident that greater equality of opportunity would produce greater equality of income. To be sure, that is not a logical necessity, and one can imagine contrary examples. Suppose the silver spoons of privileged families work mainly to lift into the middle-income range those offspring who would otherwise wind up on the low end of the distribution (but do not benefit those who would make the middle or upper range on their own). Similarly, suppose the lead weights on the disadvantaged mainly hold down those who would otherwise rise to the top, keeping them close to the middle. Under those circumstances, inequality of opportunity would serve to reduce inequality of income. But those are unrealistic suppositions. Probably, in the real world, the silver spoons aid the able as well as the inept offspring of the well-to-do; similarly, the lead weights hold down all groups of children of the disadvantaged, making car washers out of potential middle-income policemen as well as policemen out of potential high-income doctors. Under those circumstances, inequality of opportunity must increase inequality of income.[18]

Quite apart from its effect on the equality of income and on efficiency, equality of opportunity is a value in itself. Presumably it would be desirable to have fairer races. Interesting questions can be posed about how equality of opportunity should be traded off against equality of income when conflicts arise between the two. Such issues test the relative importance of the fairness of the race and the decent treatment of losers and winners. Both obviously matter. Unreasonable prizes and penalties are unacceptable, even if they are associated with fair races. The presumption that gladiatorial contests were fair made it no less barbaric to feed the losers to the lions. On the other hand, it does seem fair that losers in Olympic events go home disappointed and empty-handed. Such issues provide relaxing mental exercise, since equality of

18. Suppose an individual's income can be decomposed into two parts: A, the family advantage (or disadvantage) element; and B, everything else. On average, A is zero. The variance of $(A + B)$ must exceed the variance of B, unless A is sufficiently *negatively* correlated with B. Macroeconomists will recognize this as similar to the condition for discretionary fiscal-monetary policies to reduce the variance of GNP, which was set forth by Milton Friedman in "The Effects of a Full-Employment Policy on Economic Stability: A Formal Analysis," *Essays in Positive Economics* (University of Chicago Press, 1953), p. 123.

opportunity and equality of income are generally complementary rather than competitive objectives. That is one tradeoff that is not seriously vexing in the real world.[19]

A Meritocratic Caste System?

I am also confident that greater equality of opportunity would produce greater social mobility from generation to generation. If the impact of family advantages is reduced, so must be the dependence of the incomes of sons and daughters on those of their parents, as I have already argued. The specter that fair races will produce a hereditary caste system of meritocracy has been recently raised.[20] I regard that as farfetched. If it has any logic at all, that argument must rely on the conjecture that gearing market rewards more precisely to abilities will eliminate the lottery aspects of today's income distribution and reveal a truly hereditary elite that earns the top prizes generation after generation.[21] Such speculation is totally unsupported by evidence.

Nor is there evidence or plausibility to support the speculation that greater equality of opportunity would increase the importance of IQ differentials in the market's verdicts. There are good reasons why IQ—as distinct from educational attainment—has so little weight in the rewards of the marketplace, which reflect

19. As one example of the mental exercise, if the rate of return from education is positively related to learning ability, an equal-opportunity entry standard that screens ability perfectly will generate more income inequality than an entry standard that is an imperfect (even a mildly biased) screen. I view that as having little empirical relevance, given the tremendously biased screens that are currently used.

20. See, for example, Richard Herrnstein, "I.Q.," *The Atlantic Monthly*, Vol. 228 (September 1971), pp. 43ff. For a defense of meritocracy, see Daniel Bell, "On Meritocracy and Equality," *Public Interest*, No. 29 (Fall 1972), pp. 29–68, especially pp. 31–34. Although heredity plays a small role in his world, Michael Young predicts undesirable consequences of meritocracy in *The Rise of Meritocracy, 1870–2033* (London: Thames and Hudson, 1958).

21. This issue is perceptively analyzed in a mathematical treatment by John Conlisk, "Can Equalization of Opportunity Reduce Social Mobility?" *American Economic Review*, Vol. 64 (March 1974), pp. 80–90. After refuting the argument, Conlisk generously offers a conceivable rationale.

a wide variety of talents and efforts. Why would anyone expect business or political or most professional hierarchies to be dominated by IQ differentials in any sensible system of promotion and career evaluation? Only in academic hierarchies might IQ tend to dominate—since the test is structured in part to serve as a predictor of academic learning ability. Stress on IQ is a form of narcissism peculiar to intellectuals, and fortunately has no counterpart in the marketplace.

Races or Dances

Efforts to promote equality of opportunity accept an individualistic, achievement-oriented, and essentially competitive economy in which prizes will be given and a variety of hierarchies will continue to exist. On the other hand, some see the contests of modern society as dehumanizing rat races, and their objective is not to make them fairer but to eliminate them. They want fewer races, and more dances that feature cooperation and fraternity.[22] It may well be desirable to effect some shift in the mixture of competition and cooperation. But a major deemphasis of competition means forgoing individualistic incentives; and that, in turn, involves either a tremendous sacrifice of efficiency or else the creation of alternative incentive systems. Perhaps people will work and produce in order to serve humanity, guided by a love for all mankind as brothers and sisters. But it remains to be demonstrated that such a spirit can motivate common mortals and not merely saints. Properly indoctrinated, people can be induced to work for the greater glory of the state or of the leader of the state. Reflecting traditional values, however, most Americans would rather run races for their own prizes than run errands for their leader's glory.

---

22. For an opponent of races, see Jerome Karabel, "Perspectives on Open Admissions," *Educational Record*, Vol. 53 (Winter 1972), pp. 30–44. For a proponent of a changed mixture of races and dances, see R. H. Tawney, *The Acquisitive Society* (Harcourt, Brace and Howe, 1920), chaps. 9, 10.

Fairness and Frustration

Finally, I am confident that greater equality of opportunity need not generate more frustration. Some conservatives warn us: "Don't try it, you won't like it." As they see it, if differentials in income result entirely from differences in ability and skill, the losers will have only themselves to blame and will be unhappier than ever. Disadvantages and injustices give the losers needed excuses for their failures.

This self-serving argument, which can be traced back through two centuries, is full of holes.[23] Disparities of opportunity are currently far greater than is necessary to serve the merciful end of preserving that excuse for the losers. No batter needs to come up to the plate with two strikes to find some reason for striking out. Even if all the serious proposals for reducing inequalities of opportunity were adopted, enough disadvantages would remain to provide a convenient excuse—if that is what is needed.

Moreover, people understand the relativism of market rewards, and do not confuse the market's verdict with heaven's verdict. It is true that, in the race for dollars, all the places are announced officially—loud and clear. But when people conclude that they have run a fair race, they tend to find some sense in which they have been winners. Many participants now measure their success in dimensions other than their money incomes. Harvard professors hardly feel inferior to the president of U.S. Steel. Nor do sculptors feel inferior to college professors. The same self-respect can extend to good landscape gardeners and good plumbers, to mothers who prefer full-time home management, and to those who delegate home management in order to earn paychecks. Society can run contests without adding to frustration, so long as people engage

---

23. Blum and Kalven trace the argument through David McCord Wright all the way back to Dr. Samuel Johnson. See Walter J. Blum and Harry Kalven, Jr., *The Uneasy Case for Progressive Taxation* (University of Chicago Press, 1953), p. 90. For a modern version, see Young, *Rise of the Meritocracy,* pp. 85–87.

in many contests and use many criteria to judge their own contributions. The more criteria they employ, the more they will tend to give themselves high grades. And that is good for self-respect.

In a similar sense, there are many criteria by which social scientists can grade their own predictions and prescriptions. Those now forecasting a meritocracy of IQ will point in the future to the importance of academic talent; and they will claim victory. Meanwhile, exponents of a market society will feel vindicated because income differentials will remain important. And I confidently expect to see many scoring systems with many different rank orderings, which will validate my pluralistic views. So we will all regard ourselves as winners. And that is good for the self-respect of social scientists.

CHAPTER FOUR

INCREASING EQUALITY
IN AN EFFICIENT ECONOMY

This essay began with a visit to the domain of social and political rights in which society gives priority, at least in principle, to equality over economic efficiency. It moved into the marketplace and other economic institutions, in which efficiency gets priority and a large degree of inequality is accepted. It then inspected a few bright prospects for increasing economic efficiency and equality simultaneously. Those prospects are important, but they are limited. Frequently, society is obliged to trade between efficiency and equality. Those trades pose the difficult choices and they are the subject of this final chapter.

THE AREA OF COMPROMISE

If both equality and efficiency are valued, and neither takes absolute priority over the other, then, in places where they conflict, compromises ought to be struck. In such cases, some equality will be sacrificed for the sake of efficiency, and some efficiency for the sake of equality. But any sacrifice of either has to be justified as a necessary means of obtaining more of the other (or possibly of some other valued social end). In particular, social decisions that permit economic inequality must be justified as promoting economic efficiency. That proposition is not original,[1] but it is important and apparently remains controversial. Efficiency alone is the criterion for anyone who opposes progressive taxes because he detects some adverse effects on incentives. Equality gets no weight in the verdict of an economist who recommends the same formula for any and every shortage: let the price rise to its own level without government interference. At the other extreme, anyone who views high profits anywhere as a prima facie case for public action must be judging by equality alone.

The cartelization of the world oil market engendered a display of such pure no-tradeoff views. Free-market exponents argued the efficiency case: at a new, high, market-clearing price within the United States, curtailment of consumption and expansion of domestic production would both be encouraged. No disruptive shortages would emerge, and the limited supplies would flow to those users who needed oil most, as evidenced by their willingness to pay the most. And this argument may well have been correct, in terms of efficiency alone. But at least during the embargo, the market-clearing solution might have transferred as much as $60 billion of income (at annual rates)—a toll of $20 a week, for the average American family—from oil consumers to domestic oil producers. Wasn't some queuing at gas stations a lesser evil of inefficiency compared to that huge additional inequality?

On the other hand, the antiprofiteering hawks focused on eliminating the windfalls enjoyed by the producers rather than the shortages endured by the consumers. Although the embargo was instituted and the cartel price set by foreign potentates and not by American businessmen, the gains of a few corporations were resented, particularly because they accompanied the losses to most

---

1. See Lester Thurow, "Toward a Definition of Economic Justice," *Public Interest*, No. 31 (Spring 1973), p. 63. The germ of the idea can be found in Pigou; I suspect that it goes back a lot farther, but I can't trace it. This is a much weaker condition than Rawls' difference principle, discussed below.

Americans. In this case, what was bad for the country was unquestionably good for Exxon. Still, some of the measures espoused
(like hefty excess-profits taxes or inflexible price freezes) would
have made things less good for Exxon only by making them worse
for the country.

The actual policies adopted in 1974 lay somewhere between
the promarket and antiprofit positions. The price of crude oil for
that part of U.S. production that had been geared up by 1972
was controlled at a ceiling of $5.25 per barrel. Since the capabil-
ity for producing such "old oil" was established and expected to
be profitable when the price was $3.50, the ceiling limited the
size of windfall profits. Similarly, ceilings were set on refinery and
distribution margins. On the other hand, the price of incremen-
tal crude production—"new oil"—was not controlled and soared
above $10 to the world price fixed by the cartel. In effect, the price
of U.S. new oil was allowed to be set by OPEC, the organization
of petroleum-exporting countries, while that of old oil was fixed
by the U.S. government; neither reflected competitive forces, since
the cartel had strangled competition. The case for letting new-oil
prices soar rested on efficiency; the policy sought to generate enormous profit incentives for expanded domestic production. Considerations of efficiency and equality were thus blended into an
imperfect compromise.

In critical areas, such compromises tend to emerge from the
political process. The real question is usually one of degree. On
what terms is the nation willing to trade equality for efficiency?
Anyone who has passed a course in elementary economics can
spout the right formal rule: promote equality up to the point
where the added benefits of more equality are just matched by
the added costs of greater inefficiency. As is so often the case
with the rules that are taught in basic courses, this one provides
insight but is hard to apply to the real world. The consequences
of most redistributive measures on both equality and efficiency
are uncertain and debatable. Confronted with a proposed tax or

welfare equalization, no legislator or voter can assess how much the program would add to equality or subtract from efficiency. Thus decisionmakers do not get opportunities in the real world to test neatly their priorities between the two competing objectives. But the author of a book can create a hypothetical world that suits him. And so I can propose an experiment by which you can test your attitudes toward the tradeoff.

The Leaky-Bucket Experiment

First, consider the American families who make up the bottom 20 percent of the income distribution. Their after-tax incomes in 1974 were less than $7,000, averaging about $5,000. Now consider the top 5 percent of families in the income pyramid; they had after-tax incomes ranging upward from about $28,000, and averaging about $45,000. A proposal is made to levy an added tax averaging $4,000 (about 9 percent) on the income of the affluent families in an effort to aid the low-income families.[2] Since the low-income group I selected has four times as many families as the affluent group, that should, in principle, finance a $1,000 grant for the average low-income family. However, the program has an unsolved technological problem: the money must be carried from the rich to the poor in a leaky bucket. Some of it will simply disappear in transit, so the poor will not receive all the money that is taken from the rich. The average poor family will get less than $1,000, while the average rich family gives up $4,000.

I shall not try to measure the leak now, because I want you to decide how much leakage you would accept and still support the Tax-and-Transfer Equalization Act. Suppose 10 percent leaks out; that would leave $900 for the average poor family instead of the

2. As the redistribution is described here, the abrupt termination of the tax just below the top 5 percent of the distribution as well as of the transfer just above the bottom 20 percent would imply inequitable "notches." Any real-world proposal would have to smooth these out, and also to determine the proper sharing of the tax burden and transfer benefits.

potential $1,000. Should society still make the switch? If 50 percent leaks out? 75 percent? Even if 99 percent leaks out, the poor get a little benefit; the $4,000 taken from the rich family will yield $10 for each poor family. Where would you draw the line? Your answer cannot be right or wrong—any more than your favorite flavor of ice cream is right or wrong.

Of course, the leak represents an inefficiency. The inefficiencies of real-world redistribution include the adverse effects on the economic incentives of the rich and the poor, and the administrative costs of tax-collection and transfer programs. The opponent of redistribution might argue that my experiment obscures the dynamics of the incentive effects. He might contend that any success in equalization today is likely to be transitory, as the adverse impact on work and investment incentives mounts over time and ultimately harms even the poor. What leaks out, he might insist, is the water needed to irrigate the next crop. In addition, anyone who views market-determined incomes as ethically ideal rewards for contribution would oppose the switch, regardless of the size of the leak.

On the other hand, some would keep switching from rich to poor as long as anything at all remains in the bucket. That is the import of John Rawls' difference principle, which insists that "all social values . . . are to be distributed equally unless an unequal distribution of any . . . is to everyone's advantage"—in particular, to the advantage of the typical person in the least-advantaged group.[3]

Rawls has a clear, crisp answer: Give priority to equality. And, as he always does, Milton Friedman has a clear, crisp answer: Give priority to efficiency.[4] My answer isn't neat. My answers rarely are, and that is one trouble I generally encounter in such ideological debates. Here, as elsewhere, I compromise. I cannot accept Rawls'

---

3. John Rawls, *A Theory of Justice* (Harvard University Press, 1971), p. 62.

4. This position is clearly implied by Friedman's discussion in *Capitalism and Freedom* (University of Chicago Press, 1962), pp. 161–66, although it obviously is not addressed to my particular experiment.

egalitarian difference principle. It is supposed to emerge as a consensus of people in the "original position," when they develop social rules without knowing where their own future incomes will lie on the pyramid. But, as other economists have noted,[5] that difference principle would appeal only to people who hate to take any risk whatsoever. That is the implication of the view that no inequality is tolerable unless it raises the lowest income of the society. According to this "maximin" criterion, society is worse off if the lowest-income family loses one dollar, no matter how much everybody else in the society gains. For example, a framer of the social constitution would embrace the difference principle only if he preferred a society that guaranteed every family $14,000 a year—no more and no less—over one that provided 99 percent of all families with $20,000 and 1 percent with $13,000. Put the American people in an "original position," and I certainly would not expect them to act that way.[6]

If I were in Rawls' original position, I would argue that the social constitution should not seek to settle forever the precise weighting of inequality. It should instruct the society to weight equality heavily, but it should rely on the democratic political process it establishes to select reasonable weights on specific issues as they arise.

5. See Kenneth J. Arrow, "Some Ordinalist-Utilitarian Notes on Rawls's *Theory of Justice*," *Journal of Philosophy*, Vol. 70 (May 10, 1973), pp. 245–63; and Sidney S. Alexander, "Social Evaluation Through Notional Choice," *Quarterly Journal of Economics*, Vol. 88 (November 1974), pp. 597–624.

6. I do believe that risk aversion encourages preferences for equality. In my view, Rawls' original position provides a better framework for a behavioral interpretation of egalitarian preferences than previous attempts to derive them from interpersonal comparisons. Anyone who dislikes gambling to some degree and who doesn't know where he will land on the income pyramid would tend to prefer less inequality in the distribution of income. Moreover, I would expect civilized human beings to display some degree of risk aversion (although not an absolute aversion). I'm not convinced, however, that egalitarian social preferences must rest on personal risk aversion. Suppose a bunch of gamblers were forming a society from an original position; would they necessarily prefer a world in which the winner takes all or might they see some justice in a degree of equality?

Unlike Friedman, I would make the switch in the leaky-bucket experiment with enthusiasm if the leakage were 10 or 20 percent. Unlike Rawls, I would stop short of the 99 percent leak. Since I feel obliged to play the far-fetched games that I make up, I will report that I would stop at a leakage of 60 percent in this particular example.

If your answer, like mine, lay somewhere between 1 and 99 percent, presumably the exact figure reflected some judgment of how much the poor needed the extra income and how much the rich would be pinched by the extra taxes. If the proposed tax were to be imposed only on the handful of wealthiest American families with annual incomes above $1 million, you might well support the equalization up to a much bigger leakage. In fact, some people would wish to take money away from the super-rich even if not one cent reached the poor. And those avid redistributors are not necessarily either mean or radical. Some think such a levy might help to curb the political and social power of the Hugheses and Gettys—an argument about which I expressed my skepticism in chapter 1. Others see it as a symbolic kind of environmental program; they feel that the villas, yachts, and jets of the super-rich poison our land, water, and air. Still others are frankly envious. For any of these reasons, many would go even farther than would John Rawls.

I shall now carry that leaky bucket on one final trip, in an effort to determine attitudes about various income levels. Consider two groups of families, one with after-tax incomes of $10,000 and the other with $18,000—figures that bracket the $14,000 national mean in 1974. Suppose the proposal is to raise taxes on the $18,000 group and aid the $10,000 families by reducing the taxes they now pay. How much of a leak would you accept and still support that transfer? These families are quite far apart on the totem pole: the $10,000 family is only about three-eighths of the way up, while the $18,000 family stands four-fifths of the way to the top. I see some value in that redistribution, but my enthusiasm is limited; a leakage of 15 percent would stop me.

Somehow, everyone seems to develop a sense of where deprivation and hardship begin along the income scale. Among economists and laymen alike, the subjective threshold of deprivation most often mentioned is half of the average income of American families.[7] If the average is taken as the mean, that would run about $7,000 in 1974 (half the median would be $6,000). Filling that gap seems far more important to many reformers than narrowing disparities above that level. That attitude has very important implications for policy. Additional doses of the old tax-and-transfer compound can essentially cure the deficiency below half of average income, as I shall argue below. But they would have only limited effects on the differentials between the $10,000 and $18,000 groups. To shrink those differentials significantly would call for alternative prescriptions. In particular, society would need to find ways for more people to climb the ladder from fair jobs to good jobs by choosing some combination of various proposals for expanded formal education, enhanced vocational and manpower training programs, subsidies to employers for promoting workers within their own ranks, or an induced narrowing of wage differentials between higher and lower job classifications. These issues intrigue me. But because the bottom end of the income scale is the top of my priority list, I shall concentrate largely on the tax-transfer options.

Inspecting the Leakages

Just how leaky is the bucket? I can offer a few clues to the answer by inspecting the various inefficiencies of the tax-transfer reshuffle—administrative costs, reduced or misplaced work effort,

7. The criterion of half of average income is used in Victor R. Fuchs, "Toward a Theory of Poverty," in Task Force on Economic Growth and Opportunity, *The Concept of Poverty* (Chamber of Commerce of the United States, 1965). Lee Rainwater finds that the public's subjective attitudes correspond to this criterion. See *What Money Buys: Inequality and the Social Meanings of Income* (Basic Books, 1974), pp. 41–63, 110–17.

distorted saving and investment behavior, and possible changes in socioeconomic attitudes.

ADMINISTRATIVE COSTS. The federal government has to hire people and buy computers in order to collect taxes and to distribute transfer payments. In addition, the taxpayer bears some costs of complying with the laws, including the time spent filling out forms and the fees paid to lawyers and accountants. These are deadweight burdens of the system and they absorb resources that could be serving productive ends. But the resulting leakages are fairly small and can be reasonably quantified; only a few percent of the contents leak out in this form.

WORK EFFORT. The impact of taxes and transfers on work effort is more difficult to assess. Suppose, as a result of increased income-tax rates, an individual takes more leisure and does less work than he would otherwise; then something leaks out of the real income and output available to all the citizens combined. In that case, to give poor Paul $1, the extra tax will cut rich Richard's spendable income by more than $1, by, say, inducing him to take an unpaid vacation that he would not otherwise want. The vacation must be worth something to Richard, but not as much as the income he would have chosen had it not been for the tax hike. Whether the net loss is viewed as a cut in the potential benefit to Paul or an extra burden on Richard, it is an inefficiency. In fact, dozens of researchers have plowed into this area.[8] They have uncovered virtually no significant effects of the present tax system on the amount of work effort of the affluent.[9] Some limited

8. See, for example, George F. Break, "Income Taxes and Incentives to Work: An Empirical Study," *American Economic Review,* Vol. 47 (September 1957), pp. 529–49; the literature is summarized by Break in "The Incidence and Economic Effects of Taxation," in *The Economics of Public Finance* (Brookings Institution, 1974), pp. 180–91.

9. The absence of dramatic effects should not be surprising. It could reflect a standoff between "substitution effects" and "income effects"—the two distinct and opposite influences implied by economic theory. Higher income taxes make leisure cheaper, setting off the substitution effect of trading work for leisure. But meanwhile they induce people to work more in order to avoid a major cut in living standards, as they reduce take-home pay and hence exert an income effect.

effects of transfer payments have been found on the work effort of secondary earners (that is, ones other than the family head) in low-income families, but virtually none on primary earners.

It does not take a research project, however, to identify mis-placed—socially unproductive—efforts devoted to tax minimiza-tion. High tax rates are followed by attempts of ingenious men to beat them as surely as snow is followed by little boys on sleds. One form of misplaced effort is on-the-job luxury financed by tax-deductible business expenses. That inefficiency is evident in some uses of company airplanes and yachts, business conferences in Capri and the Caribbean, and expense-account meals in posh restaurants that thrive on soft before-tax dollars.[10] These cases seem more serious to me for their obscenity than their inefficiency. And they could be curbed significantly—although not entirely—by amendments to the Internal Revenue Code. Those amendments could tighten further the definition of an eligible deduction in the area of high living; or, instead of this stick, they could provide a carrot in the form of a standard deduction for firms that include no luxury-tainted outlays as business expenses.

At some high rate of income taxation, people might also shift their efforts toward more untaxed services of a do-it-yourself variety or switch into occupations that bestowed more untaxed rewards in the form of perquisites and amenities. But, so far as economists can see, that is not a great national trend.

SAVING AND INVESTMENT. The impact of high tax rates on the willingness to save and invest is the leakage cited most widely and confirmed least convincingly. If progressive taxation had had a massive and dominant effect on saving and investment, the evi-dence would be loud and clear in the aggregate data. In 1929, when all federal tax rates were low and barely progressive, the

10. The one effort I know that seeks to document these practices is *President's Tax Message* . . . , Submitted by Secretary of the Treasury Douglas Dillon, at Hear-ings conducted by the House Committee on Ways and Means, 87 Cong. 1 sess. (1961), pp. 177–259.

nation saved and invested 16 percent of GNP; in 1973, with all the allegedly onerous "soak the rich" taxes, it saved and invested the same 16 percent of GNP.[11] (And the evidence does not suggest that other forces, on balance, pushed up on the saving rate and hence might have offset some important downward pressures from the tax system.) Nonetheless, incessant warnings are sounded, as they have been for generations, that the next step toward greater progressivity will take saving and investment over a cliff. No doubt, the disincentive effects would become significant at some set of very high tax rates, but the terrain is a gentle slope rather than a cliff.

More fundamentally, the specter of depressed saving is not only empirically implausible but logically fake—as was the egalitarian argument of the thirties that redistribution was needed to cut saving and thus bolster consumption. Both are fakes because the nation can have the level of saving and investment it wants with more or less redistribution, so long as it is willing to twist some other dials. For example, any threat that greater progressivity would make saving inadequate could be offset by more federal saving through budget surpluses or more middle-class saving through special incentives. Similarly, investment demand could be bolstered by easing credit policies or strengthening investment tax incentives.[12]

Most fundamentally, the concern about the distortion of saving incentives through taxation implies that, with a properly "neutral" tax system, the marketplace would grind out an optimal level of saving and investment. But that is a fantasy. Collective

11. This reflects the operation of Denison's law, enunciated in Edward F. Denison, "A Note on Private Saving," *Review of Economics and Statistics,* Vol. 40 (August 1958), pp. 261–67. Paul A. David and John L. Scadding have recently confirmed its accuracy in "Private Savings: Ultrarationality, Aggregation, and 'Denison's Law,'" *Journal of Political Economy,* Vol. 82 (March/April 1974), Pt. 1, pp. 225–49.

12. One egalitarian who faces up to these issues and opportunities is James E. Meade; see his *Efficiency, Equality and the Ownership of Property* (Harvard University Press, 1965), pp. 53, 59.

decisionmaking—not the marketplace—controls the whole area of public capital formation for such diverse facilities as dams, post offices, highways, and hospitals. Moreover, investment in human capital is determined largely by public budgets for education.

The market rules investment decisions on private physical capital, but the conditions for optimality do not prevail. The market result can be optimal only if everyone faces the same interest rate, and hence can use the same scale to balance the productivity of extra investment against his time preferences for consuming more now rather than saving for later. As I emphasized in chapter 3, that neat balance is a grand illusion when some face 8 percent interest rates, others pay 36 percent, and still others cannot borrow at any price. So long as such disparities persist, there is no way to find the right national target for saving and investment in the marketplace. Decisions on how much the current generation should curb its consumption in order to bequeath more capital to future generations belong on the agenda for collective choice as clearly as does national defense policy. The only hope for the proper participation of lower-income groups in such decisions lies in voting by ballots rather than by dollars

SOCIOECONOMIC LEAKAGES. Some of the concerns about leakages from tax-and-transfer redistribution focus on adverse effects on attitudes rather than losses of real GNP. They raise a different set of questions: Do high tax rates on the affluent jeopardize the motivating influence of the rags-to-riches dream? Do they imply an adverse ethical judgment on economic success that might make talented youths ashamed to strive for the jackpot prizes? With respect to the transfer recipients, do payments that are not linked to work harm pride in self-reliance or compromise the conviction that contributing is belonging?

At the same time, questions arise about potentially favorable attitudinal effects: Does equalizing help to broaden participation in the mainstream? Does it reduce the disruptive force of envy? Can a shared concern for the poor help to unite society?

The attitudinal impacts are associated with specific kinds of leakages; and, in light of them, some leaks may be particularly worrisome—even if they imply no major loss of real GNP. For example, a desire to hold open the route from rags to riches argues for some moderation in top-bracket rates on income and estates; a concern for self-reliance and the work ethic points to the development of transfer programs that promote wage-earning activity by the disadvantaged.[13]

FILLING THE BUCKET

Through leakages, the bucket loses part of its contents. But it can still hold plenty when it reaches the deprived if it is filled in reasonable ways.

Income Taxation

The progressive income tax is the center ring in the redistributive arena, as it has been for generations. In their ten-point radical program of the Communist Manifesto, Marx and Engels put it in second place—behind only the abolition of private land ownership.[14] Yet, by 1913, that measure had become law through a constitutional amendment in this bastion of free enterprise. It was supported not only by ardent reformers but also by some middle-of-the-road groups, who saw it as a fair and reasonable way to divide the costs of public goods like the Army, the federal courts, and the regulatory commissions. Various concepts of ability to pay and of benefits of social protection were invoked to argue that a

13. My colleague Richard Nathan offered a particularly interesting personal reaction. Because he is most concerned about the dangers of a dependent class that has neither self-respect nor the respect of other citizens, he would support switches up to a much larger leakage in the leaky-bucket experiment if the leak involved mainly administrative costs and more leisure for the rich than if it were principally the result of diminished work effort by the poor.

14. Karl Marx and Friedrich Engels, "Manifesto of the Communist Party," in Lewis S. Feuer (ed.), *Basic Writings on Politics and Philosophy: Karl Marx and Friedrich Engels* (Doubleday, 1959), p. 28.

fair sharing of the tab for the federal budget required tax bills to rise more than in proportion to income.[15]

In the past generation, however, a revolution in the composition of the federal budget has rendered obsolete (or perhaps has unmasked as fallacies) these nonredistributive justifications for progressive taxation. Public goods provided by the U.S. government through purchases of goods and services have shrunk to 37 percent of the budget in fiscal year 1975, from 65 percent in fiscal year 1955. Meanwhile, transfer payments to persons (including such items as old-age benefits, Medicaid and Medicare, and welfare), which were only 18 percent of the budget twenty years ago, have shot up: they passed purchases of goods and services in fiscal 1975, and will exceed them henceforth.

Transfers are, in effect, negative taxes—payments by the government to finance spending by private citizens. They place the government squarely in the business of reshuffling incomes. In that business, it is aiding particular groups in adversity rather than providing general services to fill gaps in the marketplace. With more of total federal taxes financing transfers than financing public goods, the questions about the revenue structure can no longer be posed in terms of how society should share the bill for public goods.

The relevant issue has to be restated: Given the decision to reshuffle incomes, how should negative and positive taxes be apportioned? Tax policy should be confronted candidly as part of the decision of how much and how the government should equalize incomes. Unlike most classical writings on tax policy, Henry Simons' verdict stands up well: inequality is "unlovely," and progressive taxes are one way to reduce inequality.[16]

---

15. For a comprehensive discussion, see Walter J. Blum and Harry Kalven, Jr., *The Uneasy Case for Progressive Taxation* (University of Chicago Press, 1953).

16. *Personal Income Taxation* (University of Chicago Press, 1938), pp. 18–19. Simons attributes the concept initially to Adolph Wagner. When I invoke Simons' justification, I do not mean to imply that he would have favored as much redistribution as I do or even as much as has now been achieved.

How much, in fact, is inequality reduced by the tax-transfer reshuffle? Most of the redistribution works through transfer payments. State and local taxes are actually regressive—taking a larger fraction of incomes from the poor than from the rich.[17] Federal taxes are essentially proportional over the bottom 95 percent of families on the income scale; there, the progressive income tax is held to a draw by regressive excise taxes and the payroll tax that finances social security. For the top 5 percent of families, however, personal and corporate income taxes win the match and make the federal tax structure significantly progressive. When before-tax incomes are calculated broadly to include items treated preferentially by the tax laws, federal personal income tax bills in 1972 amounted to 11 percent of income on average for all Americans; they were 27 percent of income for families with before-tax incomes above $50,000, roughly the top 1 percent on the scale.[18]

Despite some notorious instances to the contrary, the rich and the super-rich do pay proportionately more taxes than the average American. In 1972, that top group with incomes above $50,000 paid $22 billion in federal personal income taxes. The progressive part (that in excess of the 11 percent national average tax rate) amounted to $13 billion—more than the total federal cost of Medicaid, welfare, food stamps, and public housing combined. The harvest from the progressivity of the individual income tax is not just peanuts![19]

17. See Joseph A. Pechman and Benjamin A. Okner, *Who Bears the Tax Burden?* (Brookings Institution, 1974), pp. 62–64.

18. See ibid., pp. 48–77, and also Joseph A. Pechman and Benjamin A. Okner, "Individual Income Tax Erosion by Income Classes," in *The Economics of Federal Subsidy Programs*, A Compendium of Papers Submitted to the Joint Economic Committee, Pt. 1, *General Study Papers*, 92 Cong. 2 sess. (1972), pp. 13–40 (Brookings Reprint 230).

19. The technical argument that progressive taxation is peanuts stresses the tiny shifts it produces in the Lorenz curve. That says more about the insensitivity of that curve to socially significant shifts in the income distribution than about the ineffectiveness of the personal income tax. In addition to its general insensitivity, the Lorenz curve does not reflect the much greater importance that most people attach to inequality at the extremely low end of the distribution.

The effective tax rate on extra dollars of income for even the super-rich is, however, less than half the 70 percent ceiling rate in the statutory tax brackets, in part because many types of property income are permitted to escape the tax base. Tax reformers such as my colleague, Joseph Pechman of the Brookings Institution, have alternative packages that would raise $10 billion to $20 billion a year from the income taxes of top-rung individuals and of corporations by broadening the tax base. The featured attractions of such programs are a pair of changes in the treatment of long-term capital gains. The first would increase the portion of capital gains that is included in the tax base. Under present provisions, the taxpayer adds only half of such gains in calculating his taxable income. The proposed reforms would reduce or even eliminate that discount.[20] The second provision would foreclose the escape from capital-gains taxation through bequest or gift. Taxes on capital gains are paid only when the gain is realized through a sale; transfer by bequest or gift is not regarded as a realization under present law, but would be under the reformed provisions.

No doubt, the first provision—taken alone—would encourage people to retain their big winners rather than sell them and pay the tax. And that would be a leakage. But the second would remove the present incentive for people to hold on to capital gains for dear life because the tax can be ultimately evaded when dear life ends. Removing that distortion would increase efficiency.

On another issue, I confess to my professional readers that I am deemphasizing the equalizing role of the corporate income tax because of uncertainty about its incidence; see Pechman and Okner, *Who Bears the Tax Burden?* pp. 27–39.

20. Contrary to some recent discussions, the capital-gains discount cannot be justified as an allowance for inflation. Recipients of capital gains obtain at least *some* increases in the nominal value of their assets; if they are entitled to an allowance for inflation, then it is all the more necessary for holders of cash, savings accounts, and mortgages who get no nominal gains whatsoever. So far, the tax system is based on the yardstick of the dollar, and I find that defensible. If inflation remains intense enough to justify shifting to another yardstick, then capital gains would be only one of dozens of areas in which the measurement of taxable income would have to be revamped.

Rounding out these programs are several smaller measures to curb accelerated depreciation, eliminate above-cost depletion, and discourage the issuance of tax-exempt municipal bonds. The reformers are also eager to strengthen the federal estate tax. On paper, that tax looks like a powerful mechanism for the long-term equalization of wealth, with a 77 percent tax rate on the portion of estates above $10 million. But it has holes big enough to sail J. P. Morgan's yacht through. The biggest hole is the permissive treatment of the generation-skipping trust, by which Great Grandpa can provide abundantly for his children and grandchildren while ensuring that the estate will elude taxation during their generations.

A tax-reform program can produce quite a pool of added revenues without removing provisions like the investment tax credit that have a reasonable rationale on efficiency grounds, or ones like homeowners' tax preferences that benefit middle-income as well as very-high-income taxpayers; without increasing taxes on salary incomes at all; and without any escalation of statutory tax rates. I doubt strongly that such base-broadening programs would have major leakages—say, anything more than 10 or 20 percent. They raise no threat to work effort, and they may actually reduce socially unproductive searches for loopholes. They can finance a step toward equality at a low cost in efficiency. It must be recognized, however, that if the total of national saving and investment is to stay on target, the extra revenues cannot be converted dollar for dollar into extra consumption for the poor. Probably more than half of the added taxes of the rich would come out of saving and that portion would have to be offset by more saving through federal budget surpluses in prosperity or more saving by the middle class induced by special incentives.

Redirection of Federal Outlays

To me, the purpose of heavier taxation at the top of the income and wealth scale is not to bring down the affluent but to raise up the deprived. It is one way to fill the bucket. Another way is a redirection of federal expenditures toward income-equalization programs and away from other outlays. While many programs compete for space in the budget, the sheer size of military outlays makes them the natural target for egalitarians. The debates between the military-industrial complex and the "socio-urban" complex that have frequently flared up in the past decade reflect that arithmetic as well as differences in philosophy.

Historically, the bucket has received most of its inflow from the expansion of tax revenues accompanying economic growth. That is the "fiscal dividend" that Walter Heller popularized when he was chairman of the Council of Economic Advisers in the early sixties. But when Gardner Ackley and I chaired the Council, the fiscal dividend vanished, partly because of Vietnam outlays and partly because of advance commitments to several new domestic programs with steeply rising paths of expenditures. Many of those programs have since leveled off, a few have been cut down or even phased out, and only a few new ones (most notably, revenue sharing) have been added to the list. Moreover, inflation has raised the real tax revenues of the federal government because of the progressivity of the income tax. Thus, the fiscal dividend may again rear its lovely head in a period of renewed economic expansion.[21] That could help fill the bucket in the least painful and least divisive way.

AIDS TO LOW-INCOME GROUPS

Transfer payments that flow out of the bucket are the key federal income-equalizer. They provide more than half of the available incomes of Americans below the poverty line, and lift millions more above it.

---

21. Early in 1974, the prospective room for new initiatives by 1980 was placed at $39 billion. See Barry M. Blechman, Edward M. Gramlich, and Robert W. Hartman, *Setting National Priorities: The 1975 Budget* (Brookings Institution, 1974), pp. 250–53. The Nixon health-insurance proposal was allowed for in advance of this calculation, and the inflation rate was projected at only 3 percent.

Transfers to the Aged

Transfers are especially important to the aged. Efficiency is not a serious bar to society's ensuring the right to survival at some reasonable minimum for those who cannot work because of age (or disability). It is an issue only to the extent that the detailed provisions of retirement benefits influence the termination point of working careers. Apart from that, the principal limit on benefits for the aged is the willingness of the working populace to help. In fact, society has shown some generosity to the aged (and the disabled), evidencing a genuine concern for poverty among those groups for whom work disincentives are not a major problem. To be sure, a larger proportion of the aged than of people in their working years still have incomes below the poverty line: about 16 percent compared with 9 percent. But vast increases in the level and coverage of social insurance programs are changing that story dramatically. Those retiring at age 65 currently will be below the poverty line in old age only if they have been extremely and persistently poor in their working years.

In fact, the monthly social security checks that elderly families receive today are not closely related to the payments they previously made into the system, and generally exceed by a wide margin the private annuity that those in-payments would have bought. Social security produces a huge redistribution from today's young to today's aged. But neither the government nor any private group makes a big deal out of that reshuffle. Today's young know their turn will come, and so they foot the bill without gripes. To the aged, social security benefits are a right, and so they cash those checks without guilt.

The resulting consensus about the system is its magic. Thus, in the heat of the 1972 election campaign, the Congress coolly enacted and the President quietly signed a $10 billion hike in payroll taxes. Because they are linked to the financing of social security benefits, those taxes were accepted at a time when higher taxes for anything else would have produced a new Boston tea party. In terms of public attitudes, social security is probably the greatest success of any major federal expenditure program in American history. And it has brought the nation within sight of ending poverty for the aged.[22]

The Younger Poor

The problems of the poor of working age and their children continue to plague the nation. In 1973, 4 million American families with heads under age 65 were living on incomes below the poverty line—which, for a nonfarm family of four, was drawn at $4,540. (With rapid inflation, the threshold was about $5,000 in 1974.) And poor families include 9½ million children under 18, 5½ million white and about 4 million black. Yet, the total shortfall in annual incomes below the poverty line for all people under 65 is only about $9 billion. About 9 million families with heads under 65 have incomes below the criterion of deprivation based on half of mean family income, or about $7,000. Yet, the aggregate shortfall of income below that line is only about $25 billion. Thus, much less than 1 percent of GNP would fill the entire poverty gap, and less than 2 percent of GNP could raise every family of working age to half of mean family income. Since such a program can be financed within a few years, I am tempted to declare that every working-aged American family can and should be guaranteed half the average income. A great forward stride toward equality would be taken, the right to a decent existence would be fulfilled, and this chapter would be shorter.

But the bucket is leaking again. Inefficiency makes the problem much more complex and expensive. Suppose every family of four is guaranteed a $5,000 income. Working members of families that

22. It is true that the financing of social security will become more troublesome in future decades if the growth of the labor force slows (reflecting the recent birth dearth) while the growth of the dependent aged population is maintained. But the prospects are not cataclysmic. See John A. Brittain, "The Social Security System Is Not Perfect, But It's Not Bankrupt," *Challenge*, Vol. 17 (January/February 1975), pp. 53–57.

have not been able to earn $5,000 would have incentives to quit their jobs. Why would anyone take, say, a $2,000 grant on top of $3,000 of wages, when he is offered a $5,000 grant and full-time leisure? That might even be an appealing option for many families with $6,000 (or more) earned at unpleasant jobs. That nice $9 billion poverty-eradication program could conceivably wind up costing as much as $45 billion, implying a leakage out of the bucket as high as 80 percent.

Neither poor Americans nor rich ones can be expected to work for nothing. A 100 percent subsidy—or negative tax—on any shortfall of income below $5,000 would gravely impair the work incentives of the poor, just as a 100 percent tax rate on all salaries and self-employment income above $50,000 would shrink work effort by the rich. Efficiency requires that people—rich and poor—keep a significant part of any additional income they earn. The sum of government aid and wages must be greater for the family that earns $3,000 in wages than for the family that earns none. Thus, government aid cannot be reduced dollar for dollar as earned income rises.

The poverty-eradication program has to go back to the drawing board. Now consider a new version, which still gives $5,000 to families with no earnings, but cuts benefits by only 50 cents for every dollar of wages earned. In effect, the "tax rate" on earnings is reduced from 100 to 50 percent. But then, when the family with no earnings gets $5,000, the family with $5,000 of earnings gets a benefit of $2,500, making its total income $7,500, well above the support level that was initially intended. Indeed, some aid will go to families with before-tax incomes up to $10,000, and that includes about one-third of all families. The total cost of the program has again skyrocketed.[23]

---

23. For a more detailed, systematic discussion of the problems mentioned here, see Henry J. Aaron, *Why Is Welfare So Hard to Reform?* (Brookings Institution, 1973).

Of course, I have just reinvented a variant of the McGovern demogrant plan, which proposed to give $1,000 to everyone. It then taxed earnings at a rate of one-third, so that some aid for families of four extended all the way up to incomes of $12,000. Many Americans with incomes in the $8,000 to $12,000 range who regard themselves as independent and self-supporting were insulted by the prospect of a federal dole. Even more obvious—and less surprising—was the shock of those in the $25,000 to $35,000 range who do not regard themselves as rich and yet were asked to pick up much of the bill.

Actually, McGovern's demogrant was not really revolutionary in principle. It was distinguished from the Nixon administration's original family assistance plan of 1969 mainly by its size. It was FAP viewed through a magnifying glass. That earlier program had proposed a basic stipend of $1,600 for a family of four, and a "tax rate" of 50 percent on earnings above $720, thus phasing out before income reached $4,000. That proposal fell between two stools: it was too radical in principle for conservatives (including some administration officials) and too stingy for many liberals, to whom it was an eighth of a loaf and worse than none.

At the low levels of support proposed in the family assistance plan, work incentive could not have been a serious problem. Nonetheless, the program raised an issue of principle: whether society should provide systematic cash support for people who had voluntarily opted out of its basic family and work institutions, such as the commune hippie and the unmarried mother. Many legislators wanted to require work effort—and, after all, a diligent effort to land a job is required for unemployment compensation. The applicability of the work requirement to women family heads with school-aged children raised serious issues. Some who really believed in such a requirement feared its potential incentive effects: they speculated (with no specific evidence) that if a woman were exempted from work so long as she had a pre-school child she might be more likely to have another baby when her youngest approached school age.

THE FATHERLESS FAMILY. Such issues get into the most baffling area of the poverty problem—the fatherless family. Nearly half of all poor white children and two-thirds of all poor black children live in families headed by their mother—separated, divorced, widowed, or never married. Low-income families headed by women are the principal beneficiaries of the present welfare program of aid to families with dependent children (AFDC). In 1972, more than 3 million families (nearly all of them fatherless) received over $7 billion of benefits from that program. The size of the AFDC rolls was one of the fastest-growing U.S. statistics during the sixties, doubling about every four years.[24]

Society's dilemma is much clearer than the solution to it. Generous aid removes important economic incentives that discourage women from getting into dependent positions, and that discourage their men from putting them there. But stingy aid denies the right to survival to the children of these broken families. The disincentive to the parents and the diet for the children are a tie-in sale; and that creates a particularly nasty tradeoff.

A careful and objective inspection of the "welfare" area reveals plainly that cash grants to the deprived pose genuine and difficult problems of efficiency. Callousness and stinginess are not necessarily the explanation for the present gross inadequacies of aid to the poor. But the widespread denial of benefits to husband-wife families is an incomprehensible—as well as intolerable—feature of the present system. That could be a rational choice only if this nation would rather break up five families and starve ten children than feed one lazy man. I do not believe that is the American people's true preference. It stands in startling contrast with public attitudes toward supporting the elderly, even after proper allowance for the

24. *Annual Report of the Council of Economic Advisers, February 1974*, pp. 168–69.

greater empathy that average Americans can feel for the aged than for the poor. In my judgment, the majority of the American people would be willing to pay for a federal program of cash grants for low-income families—husband-wife as well as broken ones—with the tax rate on earnings no higher than 50 percent, and with benefits that split the difference between Nixon's original FAP and McGovern's demogrant.[25]

IN-KIND AID. In addition to cash, some low-income families receive food stamps, Medicaid, housing allowances, and other aids that help them acquire specified essentials. Such aids-in-kind are sometimes opposed with the argument that the best way to help people is to give them money and let them decide how to spend it. However, entrusting unrestricted funds to parents does not ensure that children are supported. Even more generally, society may exercise a paternalistic desire to channel added expenditures toward such essentials as nutrition, health care, and housing.[26]

Aids-in-kind also have an even more basic justification; according to an argument developed by Lester Thurow but expressed in the terms of this essay, they can expand the domain of rights and help keep the market in its place.[27] For the same reasons that the poor should not be deprived of the right to equality before the law, they should not be denied decent food and medical care. Forgoing the sticks of illness and malnutrition will still leave plenty of prizes and penalties in the marketplace to provide incentives. The cliché should at last be validated: the market should not be allowed to legislate life and death. Toward that end, the forthcoming national program of health insurance should provide medical

25. This assessment of public attitudes is supported by the evidence in Rainwater, *What Money Buys*, pp. 204–17.

26. See James M. Buchanan, "What Kind of Redistribution Do We Want?" *Economica*, Vol. 35 (May 1968), pp. 185–90.

27. Lester C. Thurow, "Cash Versus In-Kind Transfers," in American Economic Association, *Papers and Proceedings of the Eighty-sixth Annual Meeting*, 1973 (*American Economic Review*, Vol. 64, May 1974), pp. 190–95.

care for low-income people at negligible charges.[28] And food stamps should remain on the menu of social assistance for those who would otherwise go hungry.

Employment Opportunities

Jobs are a key component of any program to end deprivation. The concern about work incentives and the work ethic makes sense only when it is accompanied by work opportunities. For those at the low end of the income scale, the Employment Act's pledge to provide "useful employment opportunities . . . for those able, willing, and seeking to work" must be redeemed in concrete terms. Placement, training, and employer-of-last-resort programs could be packaged to guarantee employment opportunities, at least for family heads.

The poor express willingness to work; and middle-income groups express willingness to assist the working poor. In principle, the most direct route to the goal might be a federal wage subsidy. For example, with the minimum hourly wage now set above $2, the government could fill part of the gap between below-average wages earned by adult workers and the current average hourly wage of more than $4; if the fraction were set at one-half, the minimum hourly wage received by workers would exceed $3. For a full-time, year-round job, $3 an hour adds up to about $6,000 a year, not far below the deprivation standard of half the average family income. The subsidy would help even more if combined with a reduction in the social security payroll tax for low-wage workers.

Unlike rises in the present form of the minimum wage, the subsidy would not induce employers to cut back on hiring low-wage workers. The subsidy would thus be efficient, but it would be expensive to the taxpayer. Even more fundamentally, it is anathema to labor unions, which fear that it could be the camel's nose under the tent of publicly financed business expenses, creating the

---

28. As I noted in chapter 1, that does not include an unlimited right to eyeglasses—or to cosmetic plastic surgery or to all the psychotherapy one might wish.

precedent for employers to shift more and more of their payroll costs to taxpayers. With proper safeguards against a rampaging camel, the subsidy option might become politically viable. With the present road-block, direct employment-creating efforts have put the jobs on government payrolls, mostly those of cities and states. Some of these programs have recently been quite successful on a very limited scale, probably because of their limited scale. But restricting them to the public sector forgoes the attractive potential of federal aids for building careers and raising the quality of jobs in private employment.[29]

The Politics of Equalization

The tax, transfer, and job programs that I have surveyed have been advocated for several years by people who share my values. As I see it, that makes the proposals properly aged and vintage quality—ready for consumption. When the bottles are uncorked, the contents will prove to be economically effective and politically palatable.

Why, then, haven't these programs been enacted into law? I am confident that the present structure of our tax and welfare system is not the revealed preference of the nation. For example, the Congress never intended the estate tax to be beaten by generation-skipping trusts; on the contrary, its tough intentions are clearly evident in the high tax rates it imposed. Congress enacted a package of tax reforms in 1969 that was advertised as significant but turned out to be trivial. The battle for a family assistance plan in 1971 and 1972 was lost mainly for the want of a nail of compromise.[30]

29. My skepticism about the scope of public-service employment is expressed in Arthur M. Okun, "Upward Mobility in a High-Pressure Economy," *Brookings Papers on Economic Activity* (1:1973), pp. 245–46. The case for job guarantees is argued by Arnold H. Packer, "Employment Guarantees Should Replace the Welfare System," *Challenge*, Vol. 17 (March/April 1974), pp. 21–27.

30. I do not mean to slight the other problems encountered in developing an effective and convincing program. See Alice M. Rivlin, *Social Policy: Alternate Strategies for the Federal Government*, Woytinsky Lecture No. 3 (University of Michigan, Department of Economics and Institute of Public Policy Studies, 1973), pp. 16–20 (Brookings General Series Reprint 288).

Base-broadening tax reform runs squarely into the political commandment I cited in chapter 2—that which is once given shall not be taken away. The beneficiaries of any tax break have a stronger interest in keeping it than the opponents have in taking it away. The former know all the technical aspects of the law, so they can bargain and cajole effectively. They persuade legislators by stressing the unfairness of changing the rules of the game. Thus, the real estate and securities industries guard capital-gains preferences like faithful watchdogs. And who can blame them? After all, many foundation and university officials act the same way. They get one valuable tax break from the permitted deduction of the full current market value of appreciated assets given to charity. Thus, if an old alumnus gives Harvard IBM stock that he bought decades ago for $20 a share, he can deduct many times his cost as a charitable contribution and escape capital-gains taxes. I have heard brilliant testimonials from some outstanding educators in behalf of that indefensible loophole.

Often, successful legislative reforms ride the tide of some storm that carries an issue on shore. For example, the energy crisis focused attention on depletion allowances and has set off a serious effort to reform them. Nelson Rockefeller's finances revealed the legal potential of the family trust. Richard Nixon's tax returns gave the American public a crash course on the shady possibilities of income-tax avoidance. After that education, public attitudes should be particularly congenial to a concerted tax reform that would unquestionably rule such practices out of bounds the first time around.

To capitalize on such opportunities, those who would raise the banner of equalization should also enroll in a crash course, one that studies the mistakes of their predecessors. The case made in behalf of taxing the rich and aiding the poor during the election campaign of 1972 provided an object lesson in how not to present a program of equalization to the American people. Ironically, the cause of reform received a serious setback from those who sought to advance it. With friends like that, it needed no enemies. A new effort should display more concern for the preservation of market incentives and more respect for genuine skepticism; and it should eschew divisive rhetoric. My fellow reformers should want to design programs of aid to the poor that will not spawn laziness, as they can, guided by a solid body of factual—even scientific—evidence.[31] Given their importance in the values of many middle-class Americans, opportunities for jackpot prizes should be preserved. Reformers should explore wider use of the principles of cooperation and contribution that have kept social security untainted by the suspicion of freeloading. And they should respect wealthy Americans who have won their prizes playing by the rules of the game—even as they work to raise their taxes. Equalization should have a unifying theme: this can be a better nation for rich and poor alike by fulfilling the right to a reasonable standard of decent living for all citizens.

For reasons of political feasibility as well as economic efficiency, I have emphasized new federal initiatives that operate through check writing and extending the rules of fair play, rather than programs that require the federal government to produce and deliver complex services. The former is a safer route substantively in my judgment, for reasons that I discussed in chapter 2.

But the margin of superiority is commonly exaggerated. The political climate has been chilled by disappointments about the housing, manpower, urban, and education programs of the 1960s. I believe that the main fault of those programs lay in "overpromising" rather than "underperforming." The initial prophecies of their enthusiasts set unrealistic standards by which they have been condemned. In this case, the dog got kicked because he was given such an exalted name. Those who write off all the federal efforts

31. For some important experimental results that show little or no adverse work incentives on primary earners from cash grants, see Joseph A. Pechman and P. Michael Timpane (eds.), *Work Incentives and Income Guarantees: The New Jersey Negative Income Tax Experiment* (Brookings Institution, 1975).

of the sixties leave an unsolved mystery. How do they explain the major social and economic gains made in some areas? For example, economic growth and prosperity cannot nearly account in full for the decline in the number of poor people from 40 million in 1961 to 24 million in 1969—a number that incidentally was still 24 million in 1972 before dipping to 23 million in 1973. Lyndon Johnson's domestic programs must have been doing something right!

CONCLUSION

The fulfillment of the right to survival and the eradication of poverty are within the grasp of this affluent nation. And within our vision is the target of half of average income as the basic minimum for all who choose to participate in the community's economic life. The ability of industrial capitalism to end deprivation for all has been proclaimed for generations by conservative thinkers. Just before the Great Crash, Herbert Hoover stated his goal to "remove poverty still further from our borders."[32] John Stuart Mill insisted that he would be a communist if he believed that economic misery and deprivation were inherent in a capitalistic economy.[33]

And Mill was right; they are not inherent and they can be eliminated. Indeed, in a democratic capitalism, they must be eliminated. The society that stresses equality and mutual respect in the domain of rights must face up to the implications of these principles in the domain of dollars.

I have stressed particularly the urgency of assisting the bottom fifth on the income scale and helping them into the mainstream of our affluent society. I believe that programs to help them rise

32. Herbert Hoover, in his inaugural address, March 4, 1929. See William Starr Myers (ed.), *The State Papers and Other Public Writings of Herbert Hoover*, Vol. 1 (Doubleday, Doran, 1934), p. 7.
33. John Stuart Mill, *Principles of Political Economy*, Vol. 1 (5th ed., Appleton, 1877), book 2, chap. 1, § 3, pp. 262–71.

would generate momentum through time and into wider ranges of the income scale. If those at the bottom receive the contents of the leaky bucket and are granted greater equality of opportunity, most will get on their own two feet. As I noted in chapter 3, some other social scientists are less optimistic than I am, partly because they believe that only a small part of the existing inequality of income reflects family advantages or other inequalities of opportunity. That debate cannot be settled unless and until an effort is made to equalize opportunity.

In part, my optimism reflects my standards of successful equalization. I personally would not be greatly exercised about unequal prizes won in the marketplace if they merely determined who could buy beachfront condominiums, second cars, and college slots for children in the bottom quarter of academic talent. It is the economic deprivation that blocks access to first homes, first cars, and college slots for solid students that troubles me deeply. And through the kinds of reforms I have urged, these can become available to all who want them. As Tawney stated the goal, "Differences of remuneration between different individuals might remain; contrasts between the civilization of different classes would vanish."[34]

Throughout this essay, I have sounded a recurrent two-part theme: the market needs a place, and the market needs to be kept in its place. It must be given enough scope to accomplish the many things it does well. It limits the power of the bureaucracy and helps to protect our freedoms against transgression by the state. So long as a reasonable degree of competition is ensured, it responds reliably to the signals transmitted by consumers and producers. It permits decentralized management and encourages experiment and innovation.

Most important, the prizes in the marketplace provide the incentives for work effort and productive contribution. In their

---

34. R. H. Tawney, *Equality* (5th ed., London: Allen & Unwin, 1964), p. 150.

absence, society would thrash about for alternative incentives—some unreliable, like altruism; some perilous, like collective loyalty; some intolerable, like coercion or oppression. Conceivably, the nation might instead stop caring about achievement itself and hence about incentives for effort; in that event, the living standards of the lowly would fall along with those of the mighty.

For such reasons, I cheered the market; but I could not give it more than two cheers. The tyranny of the dollar yardstick restrained my enthusiasm. Given the chance, it would sweep away all other values, and establish a vending-machine society. The rights and powers that money should not buy must be protected with detailed regulations and sanctions, and with countervailing aids to those with low incomes. Once those rights are protected and economic deprivation is ended, I believe that our society would be more willing to let the competitive market have its place. Legislators might even enact effluent fees and repeal usury laws if they saw progress toward greater economic equality.

A democratic capitalist society will keep searching for better ways of drawing the boundary lines between the domain of rights and the domain of dollars. And it can make progress. To be sure, it will never solve the problem, for the conflict between equality and economic efficiency is inescapable. In that sense, capitalism and democracy are really a most improbable mixture. Maybe that is why they need each other—to put some rationality into equality and some humanity into efficiency.

FURTHER THOUGHTS ON
EQUALITY AND EFFICIENCY

I have recently expressed in some detail my views on the goal of equality in our society, particularly in relation to the goal of efficiency.[1] I trust that it will come as no surprise to readers of this paper that I have not yet accumulated a brand-new stock of ideas, nor am I yet ready to recant. Rather, I shall use this occasion to elaborate on some of the central issues, presenting them at a level appropriate for an audience of professionals, rather than of interested laymen.

Implicit in my book (and more explicit in this paper) is a reliance on a loose notion of "revealed preferences." I look for the rationale—the internal logic—of the institutions that actually operate in contemporary American society. In moving from the realities of institutions back to the principles, preferences, and constraints that could explain them as a reasonably rational and consistent system, my chain of reasoning reverses that of the social philosopher, who starts with his principles and attempts to derive

Originally published as Arthur M. Okun, "Further Thoughts on Equality and Efficiency," in *Income Redistribution,* edited by Colin D. Campbell (American Enterprise Institute for Public Policy Research, 1977). Reprinted with permission.

1. Arthur M. Okun, *Equality and Efficiency: The Big Tradeoff* (Washington, D.C.: The Brookings Institution, 1975).

from them the practices of a "good" society. Perhaps that makes me a backward philosopher.

Yet I too am interested in the good society, and I pursue the line of revealed preferences because I think our society is pretty good. At times, however, I depart from this approach to express my personal preferences, some of which are contrary to those of the majority as reflected in the political process. Indeed, a rigorously consistent application of revealed (rational) preferences would be awfully stuffy, since it must always conclude that whatever society does is best for it, or else it would be doing something else. The theory of efficient markets often strains my credulity, and any theory of efficient institutions would shatter it. I believe I can identify accidents of history, lags and imperfections of the democratic political process, misperceptions of costs or benefits, income effects, and technological innovations that result in policies that are suboptimal or inconsistent with majoritarian preferences. But this is a tricky game, no matter how honestly one tries to play it, and the reader should be on guard for any passages in which I might seem to lean on existing practices just because I like them or to find them irrational just because I do not.

The basic observation that requires explanation is that our society accepts far more inequality in the distribution of its economic assets than in the distribution of its sociopolitical assets. In interpreting that seeming inconsistency, I shall once again argue these points:

(1) The social preference for equality applies to economic as well as to "noneconomic" assets (although the intensity of those preferences may vary among classes of items).

(2) While there may be costs of equalizing distribution in any area, those costs tend to be greater for income (and wealth) than for social and political rights. Hence, it can be rational to tolerate more inequality in the economic realm than elsewhere.

(3) The major cost of equalization of income involves the sacrifice of some of the economic efficiency associated with the unaltered determination of incomes in the marketplace.

(4) On this reasoning, inequality that is economically inefficient can be explained as rational and justified only if it serves some other social goal (liberty, respect for the market, preference for lotteries, or the like).

(5) In general, since equality of income is both desirable and costly, the optimum will involve a compromise—a sacrifice of efficiency to gain more equality than would obtain in the absence of social action, but a tolerance of more inequality than would be preferred in the absence of the costs.

(6) While various aspects of the tradeoff are amenable to economic analysis and even to empirical quantification, the optimal compromise must be sought through political decision making. And society has clearly stated its choice for that mechanism— democracy untainted by economic inequality.

THE PREFERENCE FOR EQUALITY

When an economist is asked to determine what amount of X is optimal for an individual or for a society, he immediately divides the question into two parts: (1) How much does the decision maker in question like X, in varying quantities? (2) What does it cost to get those varying quantities of X? To noneconomists, this division may appear to be an unnecessary abstraction or complication—or, as Irving Kristol has put it, a flight into "poetry or theology."[2] But it is the only way to use the tools of our trade. The strict separation of preferences and opportunities is essential in organizing the considerations that enter into rational choice.

One application of the economist's approach lies in drawing inferences about preferences from behavior with respect to close substitutes that have sharply different relative prices. Only because of a strong preference do we use any amount of the high-priced

2. Irving Kristol, "The High Cost of Equality," *Fortune*, Vol. 92 (November 1975), p. 199.

item, as we do when we put expensive gold in our teeth and TV sets, and make room for costly lobster in our diets. To a capitalistic nation, accepting the verdict of the marketplace on income distribution is the low-cost diet. That we leave considerable economic inequality on our menu is no more surprising or instructive than is the fact the individuals eat more codfish than lobster. What is striking is that our society takes some steps toward equalization, reflecting a preference for more equality of income among our citizens than the market would generate.

The underlying rationale of the social preference for economic equality has been propounded in many ways. I shall discuss briefly a few of the formulations: (1) my own technique of drawing inferences from the domain of rights; (2) John Rawls's "original position" formulation; and (3) the classical argument based on interpersonal comparisons of utility.

INFERENCES FROM RIGHTS. In our political and social arrangements, society diligently pursues equality. American institutions strive for one-person/one-spouse, one-person/one-vote, equal justice, universal freedom of speech and religion, universal immunity from enslavement, and universal and equal claims for such public services as police protection and public education. They also impose on all citizens, at least in principle, some "negative rights," or duties, such as responsibility to obey the law, military conscription when imposed, and jury service.[3]

These social and political rights reveal a preference for treating people equally. This preference is embodied in the proposition that all men are created equal, a proposition obviously intended as a social principle rather than an enunciation of a biological fact. That principle in turn fits Rawls's conception that people see equality as a type of "mutual respect . . . owed to human beings as moral persons."[4]

3. Okun, *Equality and Efficiency*, pp. 6–10.
4. John Rawls, *A Theory of Justice* (Cambridge: Harvard University Press, 1971), p. 511.

Our institutional rules suggest that the pure preference (abstracting from costs and consequences) for social and political equality is monotonic—that is, more equality is better than less, and complete equality best of all. The costs of equalization can account for society's countenancing of some inequality of rights and its failure to achieve Rawls's "lexical ordering" which would prevent any inequality of other assets from compromising equality in the domain of basic liberties.[5] In the strict sense, precisely equal justice would require every defendant at a criminal trial to have an equal chance of being represented by F. Lee Bailey. Absolute purity of equal suffrage would involve a ban on all resource-using ways of expressing partisan political sentiments. The costs of purity justify the toleration of some impurity and the adoption of criteria for practical rather than perfect equality in the domain of rights.

To be sure, a society might adopt egalitarian sociopolitical practices even though it did not have a preference for equality. If a preferred distribution with structured inequality could be obtained only by very expensive or cumbersome methods, equal rights might be adopted rationally as the less desirable but also less costly alternative—as a purely instrumental rather than a normative choice. Thus, an individual (or a society) might wish votes to be allocated according to competence or spouses according to "need" and yet despair of any satisfactory (low-cost, operational, and objective) means of achieving that allocation. In particular, such an individual or society might see a high risk that any structured inequality would be administered by government officials in ways creating distortion and discrimination among citizens.

On this argument, the nice thing about counting heads is that the calculation is so simple and objective that it defies (or at least resists) deliberate perversion by a bureaucracy. This seems to be the source of the support of equal and universal rights by some libertarians; they turn to equality only out of dire need of an objective

5. Ibid., pp. 302–303.

rule that constrains the state and the bureaucracy, or in despair of an operational rule for achieving the structured inequality they would prefer. On that line of reasoning, if there were an agreed-upon objective test of political competence, it would be used to allocate votes. I do not believe that "prediction." It is inconsistent with the way society rules out the objective test of voluntary exchange in the assignment of rights and duties, banning trades in votes, jury duty, and conscripted military service and forbidding contracts for indentured service. Deliberately, specialization and comparative advantage are ruled out of the domain of rights. There is no logical escape from the conclusion that Americans have opted for equal rights because we like equality and not because some preferred inequality is difficult to achieve.

If such a preference for equality operates in the social and political realm, it must apply to the economic realm as well. It would be hard, indeed, to imagine any set of consistent social preferences that would give great weight to each citizen's freedom of speech (or suffrage, or any other right) and none to his ability to exercise that right in the face of malnutrition or inadequate health care. Starvation would, to put it mildly, compromise "mutual respect." In practice, American society implements its preference by equalizing incomes to some degree at some costs in many ways—conferring entitlements to expensive resource-using rights like public education, imposing progressive taxation, and supplying transfer benefits in the form of social security, food stamps, and welfare. Egalitarian preferences do not—and logically cannot—stop abruptly at the boundary line between economic and noneconomic institutions. The case for economic egalitarianism can be inferred from the equality of sociopolitical rights. Of course, that inference takes as given, rather than seeking to explain, social and political egalitarianism—a delimitation of inquiry that I, as an economist, find convenient and intellectually defensible.

I would not argue that all of the economic inequality society tolerates is necessarily attributable to the perception of the costs of eliminating it. There may be a pure preference to leave some lottery—some inequality—in the income and wealth distribution.[6] Or, as I shall discuss below, there may be some value attached to the market's verdict. Moreover, the concept of complete or perfect economic equality is a will-o'-the-wisp which fortunately we need not chase.[7]

THE "ORIGINAL POSITION." John Rawls develops the general case for social, political, and economic equality by invoking a social-contract process: people in an "original position" frame a constitution in ignorance of their class position in the future society and their relative standing with respect to assets and abilities.[8] In particular, they will determine the distribution of the lottery tickets in an urn from which every individual's income will be drawn. From the vantage point of the original position, each participant must view his or her future income as a random drawing from the urn; given the absence of any clues on whether their own tickets will be high or low, all participants would be mutually disinterested. The risk aversion of individuals can then be relied on to produce a preference for equality. It can be safely predicted that the founding fathers and mothers would not design an urn that implied 50 percent probabilities of starvation and of great affluence.

I regard the "original position" as an appealing analytical device for establishing the social preference for equality. Rawls, however, goes far beyond this point by associating with that same process the "difference principle," which insists that "all social values . . . be distributed equally unless an unequal distribution of any . . . is to everyone's advantage"—in particular, to the advantage of

---

6. See the discussion of why people may like lotteries in Milton Friedman and L. J. Savage, "The Utility Analysis of Choices Involving Risk," *Journal of Political Economy,* Vol. 56 (August 1948), pp. 279–304. Their model implies local areas of increasing marginal utility in the individual's utility function.

7. Okun, *Equality and Efficiency,* pp. 70–73.

8. Rawls, *Theory of Justice,* Chapter 4.

the typical person in the least advantaged group.[9] If the difference principle (or "maximin" criterion) is intended as a prediction of how American citizens would behave in a hypothetical original position, I am confident that it is wrong. Contrary to what is implied by the difference principle, very few Americans would prefer an urn A whose tickets gave each and every family $14,000 a year to an urn B that provided 90 percent of all families with $20,000 and 10 percent with $13,900. As I interpret him, Rawls is really making a different "prediction": that, in the process of discussing the ethics under which the future society should operate, the founders would become impressed with the undesirability of taking advantage of the (unidentified) least fortunate members. Hence, they would adopt a constitutional provision against ever doing so, no matter how slightly and no matter for what benefit and return. I would doubt that prediction as well as the first (and, moreover, the principle is not ethically persuasive to me).

I would even be willing to "predict" various ways in which the original-position group would be willing to lower the minimum income in order to raise mean income, in violation of the difference principle. I suspect that they would behave in Rawlsian fashion insofar as it was necessary to insure against starvation, recognizing that the belly they fill may be their own. I would expect them to demand a large—but still finite—gain in mean income if they were to impose deprivation of a cultural (as well as a strictly physiological) character on the least fortunate members of society. There is even evidence on that issue: a sociological survey shows a widespread perception that the threshold of deprivation lies around half of the average income of the society.[10] I would expect them to show some special concern for the welfare of children. On the other hand, as I noted above, I would not be surprised if

9. Ibid., p. 62.
10. Lee Rainwater finds that the public's subjective attitudes correspond to this criterion. See *What Money Buys: Inequality and the Social Meanings of Income* (New York: Basic Books, 1974), pp. 41–63, 110–17.

even their ideal embodied some lottery; for a given average, they might prefer the majority of people to be a little below the mean so that a few could obtain some worthwhile prizes. In principle, psychologists could take some of the conjecture (and some of the fun) out of this range of issues by designing experiments in which people selected the urn from which their "living standard" would be stochastically determined for a short period—if not for the lifetime of a society.

INTERPERSONAL COMPARISONS? Both the inferences from rights and the original-position formulation are alternatives to the traditional foundation of economic egalitarianism—a foundation based on interpersonal comparisons of utility.[11] According to that line of reasoning, individuals experience diminishing marginal utility of income, as is demonstrated by their risk-avoiding behavior. When their incomes double, their economic welfare increases but does not double—as is evidenced by the fact that they will not bet their entire income double-or-nothing on the flip of a coin. If each individual experiences diminishing marginal utility of income, then the maximum utility for the whole society must be obtained when the marginal utility of all individuals is equated. And if all individual utility functions are the same, that must occur with complete equality of income.

The last assumption—that all individual utility functions are the same—is the critical one in this chain of reasoning. Since such a proposition about interpersonal comparisons of utility is not empirically verifiable, it must stand as a value judgment—all individuals should be treated as though they have the same utility functions. But that in itself is an egalitarian judgment; it "sneaks" an assumed preference for equality into the argument designed to establish that very preference. As Henry Simons once pointed out,

11. The interpersonal-comparison approach (and its doctrinal history) is discussed in Walter J. Blum and Harry Kalven, Jr., *The Uneasy Case for Progressive Taxation* (Chicago: University of Chicago Press, 1953), pp. 49–63.

that argument could prove treacherous to egalitarians.[12] Imagine a technological breakthrough in utility measurement: a new "utilometer" gives readings consistent with all other observations on any individual and yet different readings across individuals with identical incomes. The social-utility maximizers would then be committed to give especially large incomes to those citizens who are found to be efficient generators of utility. If the empty box of interpersonal comparison were ever filled, the contents might be explosive.

The appeal of the original-position approach is that it can rest its case on diminishing marginal utility without invoking interpersonal comparisons. It focuses on the way one individual would choose among urns that have large or small variances in payoffs, and relies on the well-established diminishing marginal utility of the individual to predict a preference for low variance or equality. But the "intrapersonal" comparison it requires is strained and artificial: Its "veil of ignorance" about one's own capacities introduces an element of split personality. To ensure that the participants are truly disinterested, they are not allowed to "know themselves." But that still seems analytically preferable to interpersonal comparisons.

The new egalitarian literature should render obsolete the approach based on interpersonal comparisons. Yet it is clear why the traditional approach dies hard. With interpersonal comparisons, it becomes possible to rank various Pareto-optimal states (that is, situations where no reallocation can make some better off without making some worse off) in terms of aggregate or social utility, with the higher rankings going to the more nearly equal distributions. By that standard, society misallocates resources when it distributes badly, much as it misallocates resources when it produces badly. It may then legitimately be called "waste" when the garbage of the rich contains better food than the diet of the

---

12. Henry C. Simons, *Personal Income Taxation* (Chicago: University of Chicago Press, 1938), pp. 10–14.

poor, or when more land is devoted to one private estate than to the homes of a thousand average families.

In contrast, the inferences-from-rights and original-position approaches impose on us an awkward two-stage process of defining optimality. In the first stage, those approaches must accept any and all Pareto-optimal distributions as "efficient" (in terms of preferences revealed through voluntary exchange or dollar-voting)—none involves waste. In the second stage some will be judged better than others insofar as they are more consistent with society's preference for equality—a preference that is exhibited through ballot voting and that is not readily quantifiable in dollars. The analysis must grapple with two sets of considerations—one associated with economic efficiency and the other with the preference for equality. Clearly, this is more cumbersome than the one-step approach of interpersonal comparisons—sufficiently more cumbersome to make me wish I could accept the latter. But I cannot.

THE COST OF EQUALIZATION

In our capitalistic economy, the marketplace determines the prices of factors of production—labor and various types of physical property. Given the ownership of the productive factors (which is itself strongly influenced by the market over the longer run), the factor prices in turn determine the incomes of the citizenry. That market-determined incomes provide incentives and signals that contribute to efficiency has been the main story told by the economics profession for two centuries. But market-determined incomes also generate the economic inequality we dislike. Equalizing income thus implies modifying, vetoing, or supplanting the market determination, and therein lies its cost.Doubters raise many searching questions about the efficiency of the real-world (as distinct from the competitive-model) marketplace. Does more real gross national product really mean more welfare? How seriously are consumer choices distorted by misinformers and "hidden persuaders"? How important is monopoly, which confers income as a reward for promoting scarcity rather than productivity? How serious are uncorrected externalities, excess supplies and demands? These issues are crucial, but I will ignore them in this paper—because they are so broad and complex.

All in all, I find the efficiency arguments in favor of the marketplace persuasive. These arguments have both a static and a dynamic component—getting the right things produced today and achieving progress tomorrow. The dynamic component can be further split into two parts: the importance of market incentives to accumulate physical capital (save and invest) and to innovate. I see the dynamic considerations as more important than the static considerations, and innovation as far more significant than accumulation.

Indeed, I believe that concern about accumulation incentives is grossly overemphasized in debates on redistribution.[13] The national saving-and-investment rate is, in fact, a result of political decisions—and should be explicitly faced as such. Society can have the saving-and-investment rate it wants with more or less inequality of income, so long as it is willing to twist some other dials, involving the capital-building component of public budgets, the mix of fiscal-monetary policy, and the taxation of middle-income savers and investors. In the area of innovation, collective action (such as publicly financed basic research) is essential to rescue the market from the appalling inefficiency of private property in knowledge.[14] Yet the market does provide vital incentives for experimentation and innovation that cannot be replaced on a collectivized basis. That is where the really large dynamic costs of any drastic income redistribution are likely to be found.

The basic technique of redistribution actually employed in our society lies in the tax-transfer reshuffle. It appeals to me in principle

13. Okun, *Equality and Efficiency,* pp. 98–100.
14. Ibid., pp. 57–60.

and in practice. It allows a first-round distribution of income that is dictated by market verdicts and then modifies the results by imposing progressive taxation and by supplying resource-using rights (public goods) to all and transfer benefits (the equivalent of negative taxes) to the poor. With very few exceptions, this second-round redistribution cannot be carried out costlessly: as I like to put it, we can transport money from rich to poor only in a leaky bucket.[15] Some obvious leakages include administrative and compliance costs of implementing both tax and transfer programs, altered and misplaced work efforts resulting from them, and distortion of innovative behavior as well as saving and investment behavior. The most insidious attacks on an equalization program are those that view the discovery of any leakage as prima facie evidence against the desirability of the program. Holding it up to a standard of perfection, or zero leakage, guarantees a negative verdict. A social preference for equality implies a willingness to pay some costs for equalization.

Given (1) a social preference for equality (or at least for more equality than market-determined incomes provide), and (2) a cost of altering the market-determined distribution, society faces a tradeoff between equality and efficiency. The resulting optimum will normally be a compromise.[16] Some efficiency will be sacrificed by altering the market's verdict through a second-round redistribution in the direction of greater equality. But some economic inequality will be left because it preserves economic efficiency (or some other social value, a point discussed below). Thus, society will carry the leaky bucket to pursue equality up to the point

15. Ibid., pp. 91–95.
16. In principle, the possibility of a "corner optimum" cannot be ruled out. If the cost of even the first dollar's worth of redistribution exceeded the benefits of its added equalization, zero redistribution would be optimal. At the other extreme, if the benefits of eliminating the last dollar's worth of inequality exceeded the costs of doing so, zero inequality would be optimal. Neither of these extremes appears to have any empirical relevance, unless one invokes a "principle" against any redistribution or any inequality.

where the added benefits of more equality are just matched by the added costs of lesser efficiency.

These formal principles have significant implications. For one thing, they put into perspective the often-asked question, "How much equalization of income is enough?" That issue is no different from how large a capital stock or how large a police force or how large a computer is "enough." For all, the optimal "enough" is reached when the next unit costs more than it is worth. So long as benefits and costs are continuous, both fanaticism and complacency about equalization are ruled out of bounds. Second, the principles supply sufficient grounds for society's acting to alter the results of the income distribution. In particular, the preference for equality implies that the overall tax structure must be progressive and not proportional.[17] As Henry Simons suggested long ago, the case for progressive taxes rests on the proposition that inequality is "unlovely."[18] In principle, the necessary and sufficient case for the tax-transfer reshuffle is that simple.

The formal rules do not prescribe what public policy ought to do, but they strongly suggest what public policy questions the country ought to discuss. First, the political dialogue should focus explicitly on the intensities of social preference in favor of equality: I wish that the opinion researchers would give us the public's answers to my leaky-bucket experiment. Second, economists and other social scientists should be striving to measure the leakages and the effective equalization accomplished by various programs of taxation, transfer benefits, and public goods. The effort to quantify the tradeoff ought to cover not only existing programs but also such proposals as guarantees of job opportunity, subsidization of low wages, and new forms of subsidy to higher education.

As I read the serious empirical studies of the larger and better-established programs of taxation and income maintenance, I am

17. Again, this assumes that there will be no corner optimum.
18. Simons, *Personal Income Taxation*, pp. 18–19.

impressed by the small size of the leakages they find; often 80 or even 90 percent of the contents seem to stay in the bucket. I am also encouraged by the evidence that the programs can be made even more efficient; there are opportunities to plug some of the leaks. Understandably, the leakages seem especially small for aid to the aged, where disincentives to work are not a serious problem. The major leakages in our present old-age security program seem to be confined to its options for early retirement and its structure of minimum benefits (which subsidizes groups like federal workers that do not contribute during most of their careers).

One of the key unsettled empirical issues involves the effects of education on both productivity and wage differentials. The "human capitalists" and the "screeners" in the profession have been slugging it out for years on the social productivity of educa-tion.[19] According to either view, a national increase in education reduces the dispersion of labor incomes. But the size of the leakage from such a route to equality depends on how much the invest-ment in education raises productivity. On that issue, the human capitalists are optimistic, while the screeners paint the bleak pic-ture that the investment serves mainly private ends by providing a job-screening device based on relative education. The recent work of Tinbergen offers impressive evidence on the responsiveness of differentials between the wages of the skilled and the unskilled to increases in the supply of educated workers.[20] As he suggests, a policy of saturation of human capital—investment in human capital that is overinvestment relative to any efficiency criterion—may be an important option for reducing the inequality of labor income. Still, the size of the resulting leakage depends on the relative importance of human capital and screening—an issue on which much more research is needed.

19. See the discussion in Paul Taubman and Terence Wales, *Higher Education and Earnings* (New York: McGraw-Hill, 1974), Chapters 1, 2, 9.
20. Jan Tinbergen, *Income Distribution: Analysis and Policies* (Amsterdam: North-Holland, 1975).

As Jan Pen said in his review of my book, "A quantitative guess about the rate of transformation between efficiency and equality still seems beyond the intellectual capacities of our profession. . . ."[21] He is right that this was an especially "sketchy" part of my book; I claim no special expertise in the measurement of leakages or benefits. Hence, my main message remains an appeal to the public and to the profession to sharpen the focus on the tradeoff.

THE PUZZLE OF INEFFICIENT INEQUALITY

By the reasoning above, since inequality and inefficiency are both undesirable, society should not be expected to tolerate an arrangement that exacerbates both (unless the arrangement happens to promote some other social goal). Yet, there are uncorrected situations that contribute to both inequality and inefficiency. One of the clearest and most significant is the disadvantage low-income citizens suffer in access to capital. Clearly, the poor face effective interest rates higher than those faced by the rich. This inequality in turn increases the inequality of the income distribution, particularly by discouraging investments in human capital by the poor.[22] The discrimination by lenders can arise from their natural self-interest—the invisible hand; it does not necessarily reflect any intended bias on their part. The risk to the lender depends on the borrower's total ability to repay, on the reliability of his signature. Hence, to the lender, a loan to a low-income person is riskier than one to a high-income borrower, even if the former is proposing to use the money for a project with a distinctly higher probability of success. But the risk to society lies in the use of resources for unproductive projects, and this is quite separate from the question

21. Jan Pen, "Review/Equality and Efficiency: The Big Tradeoff," *Challenge*, Vol. 18 (January–February 1976), p. 61.
22. Okun, *Equality and Efficiency*, pp. 79–82.

of whether the lender is repaid. Thus, a socially efficient allocation of capital would require that funds flow to the particular projects that are most likely to succeed, regardless of the wealth of the prospective entrepreneurs. The market's result, therefore, involves misallocation—inefficiency as well as inequality.

Why does society tolerate such a source of additional inefficiency and additional inequality? Surely, the discrimination does not promote other social values. Indeed, it is not condoned: witness the hortatory speeches by public officials asking bankers to take care of the poor; consider the specific social programs designed to ameliorate this bias—the Federal Housing Administration, Small Business Administration, student loan programs, and the rest. I think that the real answer lies simply in the limitations of public-sector technology: it is not easy to design effective, low-cost, public programs that would improve the access of low-income groups to capital. Innovations by social scientists in this area could help to reduce both inefficiency and inequality.

The more complex case of job discrimination based on race or sex presents similarities as well as instructive contrasts to discrimination in the access to capital. Both biases misallocate and distort investments in human capital. For example, the woman who knows she will be unlikely to get a management job has no incentive to invest in training to qualify as a manager. But the effect on income inequality of job bias is not necessarily as pronounced as the effect of the lending bias. Because disadvantage in access to capital is geared directly to low income and low wealth, it must increase inequality; that need not be the case for ethnic job discrimination. For example, the average income of Jews exceeded that of other Americans at times when anti-Semitic job discrimination was widespread. In such exceptional cases, equalizing opportunity (and enhancing other social values such as fairness) may actually increase the inequality of income.

Furthermore, job discrimination (unlike the lending bias) could conceivably be "perfect," in the same sense that monopolistic price discrimination can be perfect, altering distribution but avoiding inefficiency and leaving social surplus intact. Under conditions of perfect job discrimination, blacks and women (and other victims of prejudice) would get exactly the same jobs they would obtain if not disadvantaged but would merely receive less pay for them. In fact, however, the prevalence of exclusion from good jobs (rather than exploitation involving lower wages) as the technique of discrimination makes substantial inefficiency a by-product of inequality.[23]

Finally, unlike the case with lending, some people must have preferences for discrimination when job selections are biased sexually or ethnically.[24] Those discriminators obviously lost welfare when legislation enforcing equal employment opportunity was enacted, at the same time that real GNP was increased and the welfare of the victims of discrimination was enhanced. But I do not believe that the legislation should be interpreted as the embodiment of a new conviction that the welfare gained by others outweighed the welfare lost by discriminators. The legal ban on stealing a loaf of bread does not imply a judgment that the bread stealer would gain less utility than would be lost by the potential victim. The relevant social judgment is that he would be violating the rights of others and that his own utility from such activity should be disregarded. Indeed, any system of law involves decisions that certain types of preferences are inadmissible elements in a social utility function and should not be allowed to influence allocation. The political decision outlawing job discrimination reclassified preferences for discrimination as inadmissible—placing them with preferences in favor of bread stealing. By that interpretation, an

23. Taking account of such dynamic influences as the costs and benefits of education and training, I doubt that long-run "perfect" job discrimination is possible; but I also doubt that any perfectly discriminating monopolist can avoid dynamic inefficiency in the face of long-run substitution options.

24. So-called statistical discrimination may provide an exceptional unintended rationale for job bias. For example, an employer finds that women statistically have higher quit rates and he gives preference to applicants who are likely to have low quit rates.

appraisal of the social pluses and minuses of equal employment opportunity should not subtract from its total benefits the welfare loss imposed on those with preferences for discrimination. But here again the technology for ruling out such preferences is sorely inadequate, as is evidenced by the inefficient reliance on job quotas for implementing equality of employment opportunity.

In general, a clear case of inequality of opportunity emerges whenever anyone who comes to the marketplace is confronted with a "specially" unfavorable opportunity locus because of his or her personal characteristics rather than any peculiar properties of the package that he or she is offering to buy or sell. Insofar as that discrimination is practiced "imperfectly" and operates to push the person to the lower part of the income distribution, it contributes to both inequality of income and inefficiency of allocation. Wherever the social technology is available, rooting out such inequalities of opportunity offers a promising improvement in both equality and efficiency.

To the extent that inequality of opportunity breeds both inequality of income and inefficiency, there is a clear case for corrective social action that does not depend on a distinct preference for equality of opportunity. Yet, of course, society does have such a preference—a desire for fairness—which reinforces the case for correction. The social goals include both equalizing opportunity and equalizing results. Most Americans would agree that even fair races should not result in inhumane penalties on losers or unreasonable prizes for winners. In any case, the achievement of reasonable equality of opportunity in our society requires narrowing the inequality of results in which the current inequalities of opportunity are so deeply rooted.

THE RELATIVISM OF THE MARKET'S VERDICT

Throughout the analysis this far, I have assumed that citizens have preferences about the results of the economic process—the distribution of command over goods and services—that are distinguishable from their feelings about the method by which those results were obtained. This is a crucial assumption. Indeed, every serious analysis that urges society to cease modifying the income distribution is based on the contention that the market method is so good, or any method of modification so bad, that the market's verdict should be left intact.

In some important noneconomic areas, we do regard whatever results emerge as untouchable, because they are generated by an explicitly accepted ideal process. I do not believe that the winner of an election is always the best candidate, but I believe that it would be wrong to overturn the results. Similarly, I do not care whether a jury finds a particular defendant guilty or not; I care only that justice be done. And I am prepared to respect the jury's verdict, unless I learn that the intended process was violated by tampering or the like.

Unlike the jury's verdict, the market's verdict is not accepted as necessarily ultimate. The second-round "reshuffle" is established precisely to allow political decision making to second-guess the market. As revealed by our laws, the first-round process is not regarded as sacred, nor the second-round process as sinful.

THE MARKET AS IDEAL. To be sure, generations ago the marginal productivity theory of factor pricing was invoked by some economists to demonstrate the justice of the income distribution generated by a competitive market economy. I know of no proponent of that view within the economics profession today (though Milton Friedman is ambivalent).[25]

---

25. See Milton Friedman, *Capitalism and Freedom* (Chicago: University of Chicago Press, 1962), pp. 161–65. For a sampling of libertarian authors who explicitly reject the ethical rationale for income distribution based on marginal productivity, see Frank H. Knight, *The Ethics of Competition and Other Essays* (New York: Harper, 1935), pp. 54–58; and F. A. Hayek, *The Constitution of Liberty* (Chicago: University of Chicago Press, 1960), pp. 93–100.

That normative view dissolved in recognition of the enormous distinction between effort and output, of the accidental ("unmerited") variations in the value of marginal product stemming from shifts in demand, and of the dependence of each unit's marginal product on the inputs of other units, which implies the omnipresence of joint inputs (and really makes the social environment a basic joint input in everybody's production process). These considerations effectively rule out the attribution of merit or desert to the market outcome. The results of the first-round income distribution cannot be defended as fair rewards for personal contribution.

The concept of reward for contribution has an even more fundamental defect. It is the logic—perhaps the magic—of capitalism to make distribution a by-product of production; the value of products determines factor prices which in turn determine incomes. Thus, the value of extra marketable output created by the labor and property inputs of any producer is supposed to be returned to that producer in the form of command over marketable output. In that sense, each contributor takes out what he puts in; and it all appears very natural, very fair, and almost inevitable. But that appearance is convincing only in the narrow cultural context of a market economy.

Until the seventeenth century, productive contribution was not viewed as the key to income distribution. For militaristic, marauding, and slave-owning societies, the name of the game was obtaining command over goods and services without engaging in the labors of production. In both feudal and monastic societies, the carving up of the pie was governed by rules and customs that did not have much to do with contributions to the baking of that pie. Across the range of human societies, the penalty for slackers was often ostracism, physical punishment, or the threat of divine retribution, rather than deprivation from consumption. The notion that income rewards geared to productive contribution is a natural or self-evident principle is a symptom of market myopia; an excellent treatment for that disease is a careful reading of the works of Karl Polanyi.[26]

An appreciation of the relativism of market rewards can also be gleaned from contemporary noneconomic institutions. Students, soldiers, amateur athletes, club members, friends, and family members are not rewarded with a command over resources geared to their contribution to the "output" of the relevant community. The laissez-faire market economy is unique in presuming that people should take out the value of what they contributed.

THE SPECTER OF THE STATE. Most contemporary arguments that oppose altering the market's verdict do not rely on enthusiasm for the market, but instead stress the negative aspects of the political second-guessing process. Rather than deifying the market, these theories vilify political decision making. Such arguments are deeply rooted in basic philosophical conceptions of the desirable role of the state. Two modern laissez-faire theories, developed by Friedrich Hayek and by Robert Nozick, can serve to illustrate the nature of the critical issues in this huge area.

According to Hayek, the function of government is to root out the evil of coercion, but the only way it can carry out that mission is "by the threat of coercion. Free society has met this problem by conferring the monopoly of coercion on the state and by attempting to limit this power of the state to instances where it is required to prevent coercion by private persons."[27] Moreover, except in the case of the monopoly of an essential service, market arrangements do not involve coercion, according to Hayek: they

26. See Karl Polanyi, "Our Obsolete Market Mentality," in George Dalton, ed., *Primitive, Archaic, and Modern Economies* (Boston: Beacon, 1971), esp. pp. 65–67; and *The Great Transformation* (New York: Farrar, 1944; Boston: Beacon, 1957). Another type of historical perspective on the evolution of market ideology in the nineteenth and twentieth centuries is provided by R. A. Gordon, "Adam Smith in the Twentieth Century," in Leonard S. Silk, ed., *Readings in Contemporary Economics* (New York: McGraw-Hill, 1970), pp. 37–44.

27. Hayek, *Constitution of Liberty*, p. 21.

may impose hardship on individuals but not "true coercion."[28] Hence, any policies requiring coercion by the state to mitigate such noncoercive hardships would be improper, since they would serve purposes other than preventing coercion by private persons.[29] In Hayek's view, it is clearly appropriate for the citizens to authorize coercion by the state to keep them from killing one another: but it is wrong to empower the state to exercise coercion in order to prevent death by starvation that is imposed impersonally by the market. Our society is not impressed by that distinction, and neither am I.

In his presentation of the case against redistribution, Nozick offers an even more restricted concept of the desirable role of the state. He develops an invisible-hand explanation of the state: it arises from individuals hiring protective agencies to help enforce their rights; as a result of economies of scale, a single protective agency becomes dominant in the territory and thus achieves a monopoly position. Such a state could emerge "without violating anyone's rights," and only such a state can be justified.[30] The resulting "entitlement theory" of distributive justice makes the appropriateness of any distribution of assets depend entirely on the justice of their acquisition and transfer, and not at all on the dispersion of material welfare among individuals.[31]

Like John Locke, Nozick depends heavily on a concept of natural rights. Indeed, he concedes candidly that, to him, it is an assumption rather than a conclusion that "there is some set of principles obvious enough to be accepted by all men of good will, precise enough to give unambiguous guidance in particular

28. Ibid., pp. 136–38.
29. Hayek even manages to justify public services (and the coercive taxation to finance them) as coercion to prevent greater coercion: "We need only remember the role that the assured 'access to the King's highway' has played in history to see how important such rights may be for individual liberty." Ibid., pp. 141–42.
30. See Robert Nozick, *Anarchy, State, and Utopia* (New York: Basic Books, 1974); a brief summary is presented on pp. 118–19.
31. Ibid., pp. 150–53.

situations, clear enough so that all will realize its dictates, and complete enough to cover all problems that actually will arise."[32]

That assumption about natural principles or laws is indispensable to Nozick's theory. The state obviously punishes people for breaking rules. Such law enforcement can be noncoercive (not violating anyone's rights) only if the rules are "natural"—prior to and independent of the state. Thus, it can be argued that, because of natural rights, no one has the right to steal property from his neighbor: hence, when the government enforces laws against theft, it is not infringing on any right.

Frankly, I find the natural-law approach mind-boggling. One of the many questions that mystify me is how John Locke and his disciples acquired the franchise for stipulating the set of natural laws. (Was that "just acquisition"?) Suppose, for a moment, that some intruder into this game advances, as a principle "obvious enough to be accepted by all men of good will," that no citizen of an affluent society should ever be seriously deprived of material sustenance. Thus he can claim that the state is merely enforcing natural law when it carries the leaky bucket. On what basis can he be told that he is wrong? More generally, why should natural laws restrict the state's function to that of a protective association, rather than including a role as an insurance association or a mutual benevolent association?

VARYING NORMATIVE ATTITUDES TOWARD THE MARKET. Empowering the political process to second-guess the market does not imply complete neutrality—a purely instrumental attitude— toward the market. People can have preferences about the dispersion of incomes and still have preferences about the process by which income is obtained. Clearly, many Americans are market fans, who like a recognition of success that takes the form of additional command over material output; others are offended by

32. Ibid., p. 141.

the reliance on greed and competition, rather than fraternity and cooperation, as the key motivating forces in economic life.

The market fans would pay something (but not an unlimited amount) in terms of both efficiency and equality to extend the scope of market determination, while the others would make some sacrifice to narrow it. My own value judgments come out essentially neutral: I like the impersonality of the market process, and I become attached to instrumentalities that work well, but I have some negative feelings about greed and competition.

I prefer exceptionally good plumbers to average plumbers—no matter whether they are better because they are more energetic, or better trained, or better endowed genetically. But I personally want average plumbers to get less steak and smaller homes only insofar as such a structure of rewards and penalties elicits better productive performance. I believe, nonetheless, that the majority of my fellow citizens are market fans. Popular expressions of concern about work incentives, handouts, and welfare ripoffs go beyond regrets about waste in the tax-transfer reshuffle, implying some attachment to the market's principles of distribution. Suppose, for example, that the voters were offered two alternative programs that would achieve exactly the same total GNP with the same income distribution. Program A would increase transfer benefits, while program B would establish an inefficiently large subsidy for the training of unskilled workers, thus permitting some of them to earn higher pay in the marketplace. Even if it could be demonstrated that the two involved the same government expenditures, the same tax burdens, and the same leakages, I would predict that program B would be preferred by an overwhelming majority—both of those who would be taxed to finance the programs and of those who would be recipients of the benefits. Equalization that raises the wage income of the poor is more popular than transfers unconnected to work effort, and it would remain so even if it were demonstrably no more efficient.

The development of such attitudes is easy to understand. Once our laws permit affluence and poverty to coexist, our attitudes must allow the wealthy to enjoy their rewards without personal guilt and must countenance the poverty without social guilt. We become committed to make a judgment that the rich and the poor deserve what they get, or else we would feel morally obliged to narrow the disparities. In effect, the rules of the game legitimatize inequality and, at the same time, reinforce pecuniary incentives with invidious socioeconomic distinctions between productive and unproductive citizens. When it rewards success in the marketplace with social approval as well as with affluence and penalizes failure with social disapproval as well as with deprivation, society marshals a broad set of incentives for market-oriented behavior.

The market ethic has been sold to a mass market. Getting paid is "belonging" in the minds of most citizens. Sociological studies reveal that the poor really do want to work and would strongly prefer higher incomes that come from better-paying jobs rather than from more generous transfer benefits.[33] The surprisingly small disincentive effects of some income-maintenance programs may reflect the motivational force of the market ethic. That, in turn, cuts two ways. On the one hand, fairly generous transfers can be provided without encountering major leakages. On the other hand, the more general and generous the transfer programs become, the more nonmarket income is legitimized, thereby ultimately weakening the market ethic and increasing the size of the leakages. By that reasoning, welfare checks delivered with a smile may be a dangerous product. Indeed, many affluent voters want to keep the frown in transfers that go to people who, in principle, could work. On the other hand, the careful design of a contributory theology—even mythology—in old-age insurance keeps the frown out of that program, as seems appropriate for recipients

33. Leonard Goodwin, *Do the Poor Want to Work?* (Washington, D.C.: The Brookings Institution, 1972), p. 112.

for whom work disincentives are not a serious problem. Whether or not he shares them, no egalitarian can afford to ignore these market-oriented ethical attitudes when designing and promulgating proposals for carrying the leaky bucket.[34]

DECENTRALIZATION AND FREEDOM

Beyond the realm of economic efficiency, the market serves a valuable function by diversifying power in the society and, in particular, by providing a counterweight to the power of the state. Following the principles of portfolio diversification, a sound and viable society will not put all its eggs in one basket. It will rely on many mechanisms for decision making, including the formal political process, informal voluntary associations, and organized systems of nonmonetary awards, as well as the market. That is, society strives for balance: giving the market its place and at the same time keeping it in its place.

TRADEOFF WITH LIBERTY? By providing for diversification and decentralization, the market contributes to personal liberty. I attach great importance to this contribution, as should be evident in several passages in my book.[35] But I do not see a general tradeoff between equality and liberty, so long as equalization is pursued through the tax-transfer reshuffle and the other mechanisms that I recommend—which do not include extended government control over employment or greater public ownership of the means of production. In insisting that the second-round redistribution need not compromise liberty, I believe that I am making the same distinction that Henry Simons intended in the following passage: "What is important, for libertarians, is that we preserve the basic processes

34. Although I mentioned this range of issues in *Equality and Efficiency* (pp. 48–49, 100, 116), I now think they deserve even greater emphasis. I have benefited from the comments of Daniel Yankelovich at the Public Affairs Outlook Conference of the Conference Board (New York, March 17, 1976).

35. Okun, *Equality and Efficiency,* pp. 21–22, 38–40, 60, 119.

of free exchange and that egalitarian measures be superimposed on those processes, effecting redistribution afterward and not in the immediate course of production and commercial transactions."[36] Yet, I have been frequently criticized for my position on this issue. As Irving Kristol put it, ". . . the more fundamental antithesis, the real tradeoff, is not between equality and efficiency but between equality and liberty."[37] I believe that this disagreement is rooted in a confusion between liberty and private property rights.

Of course, the size and scope of redistribution affect the level of tax rates in our society (just as do the size of the defense and highway budgets). And, in a meaningful sense, higher tax rates narrow the scope of private property rights. At one extreme, absolute rights to private property imply zero taxation; and, at the other, 100 percent taxation is just a polite description of confiscation. Thus, there is a tradeoff between the size of the tax-transfer reshuffle and the scope of private property rights.

But even by the libertarian's "negative" definition of liberty "the absence of . . . coercion by other men"[38]—maximum liberty cannot be equated with the maximum scope of private property rights, inasmuch as the latter extends the police power of the state. Private property rights are exercised through voluntary exchange in the marketplace, which in turn depends critically on the state's enforcement of contracts. To be sure, contract enforcement may be viewed as refereeing rather than policing, because it "merely" requires people to abide by their own voluntary decisions. That is a valid distinction, although it must be applied consistently: if laws that require voluntary exchange to be based on truthful

36. Henry Simons, *Economic Policy for a Free Society* (Chicago: University of Chicago Press, 1948), p. 6.

37. Kristol, "High Cost of Equality," p. 200. See also James Grant, "Government in Exile? The Brookings Institution Wields Tremendous Clout," *Barron's*, Vol. 55 (October 27, 1975), p. 17; and M. Bronfenbrenner, "Book Reviews, Equality and Efficiency: The Big Tradeoff," *Journal of Economic Literature*, Vol. 13 (September 1975), pp. 917–18.

38. Hayek, *Constitution of Liberty*, p. 19.

statements do not trespass on liberty, then regulations for accurate labeling and advertising, as well as the legal enforcement of contracts, are exonerated from the charge of trespass.

The major exercise of coercion by the state applies, however, to people who are not party to the particular contract. The protection of private property rights—the enforcement of the "Keep-Off" sign—is the most pervasive encroachment on liberty (in the sense of minimum coercion) in our society. I want the state to exclude everyone else from the use of my toothbrush, and I would crusade for laws enforcing the private ownership of toothbrushes, but I must concede that such laws represent an extension of coercion by the state. However justified and self-evident the case for promarket coercion may be, it is still coercion. The inability of some libertarians to recognize coercion when it is exercised in behalf of the market is an incomprehensible blind spot in their analysis.

The conflict between liberty and private property is dramatically evident for those private property rights that are created out of thin air by the state—patents and copyrights, common-carrier and broadcasting certificates, and, most significantly, the limited-liability joint-stock corporation. I favor all of these useful institutions, but they all extend the exercise of coercion by the state. When the government grants an exclusive patent to one agent for a promising new antibiotic like Minocin, it is broadening the scope of private property rights; but it is imposing coercion on everybody else—on 99.99999953 percent of the population. By comparison, when the government bans the sale of a dangerous chemical like Kepone, it removes a private property right, opposite to the Minocin case; and it applies coercion to 100 percent of the population—only trivially different from the former case. Clearly, if all society cared about was maximizing liberty (minimizing coercion), the state should keep its hands off both Minocin and Kepone.

The cases of the altered and unaltered income distribution are to me like the Kepone-Minocin pair in these respects: the altered distribution significantly narrows the scope of private property, but does not significantly enlarge the scope of coercion. The trade-off arises between the maximum scope of private property rights on the one hand and both liberty and equality on the other, not between liberty and equality.

Maximizing the scope of private property does not maximize efficiency any more than it maximizes liberty. Within even the narrowest purview of the most abstract model of a competitive economy, efficiency requires public actions to deal with externalities, public goods, pervasive economies of scale, and incentives to destroy competition. The scope of private property rights is clearly reduced by even these minimal requirements, like public ownership of lighthouses and navigable rivers, smoke-abatement action, antimerger legislation, and regulation of the telephone company.

In my view, we can afford to deal pragmatically with the modifications of property rights required both to enhance efficiency and to increase equality, so long as the balance between the political system and the market system stays in the zone that ensures decentralization. When technology opens new areas of potentially important externalities (like the noise of SSTs and the locations of nuclear power plants), and when our affluence and our attitudes enlarge the tax-transfer reshuffle, a gradual expansion of the scope and size of the public sector is a rational response that leaves us well within the safety zone.

DEMOCRACY, DISCRETION, AND DEMAGOGUERY

There is no Lorenz curve that I or anyone else could unveil as the optimal target for the society. I was not bashful about spelling out my personal preferences in my book, although there is no reason why they should appeal to others. I do, however, hope to persuade others to share my views about the preconditions for optimization—a more focused public dialogue on the intensities of preferences for equality and a greater research effort by social scientists on the measurement of the leakages. In short, I am pleading for us all to face up to the tradeoff between equality and efficiency.

In aiming for a crystallization of social attitudes toward the tradeoff and in aiming for their implementation, I am counting on effective, enlightened, democratic political decision making. I am well aware that such a course has its dangers.

One is the danger of big and erratic changes in the rules of the game. In a majoritarian political system with two political parties, the tax-transfer reshuffle and the scope of resource-using rights might undergo a drastic overhaul whenever power changed hands. Extreme uncertainty about the future levels and progressivity of taxes, for example, could pose a serious threat to efficiency. Moreover, abrupt shifts would raise questions of fairness to those people who had accumulated wealth with a reasonable expectation that the general levels of taxation imposed on property income and wealth transfer would continue.

Obviously, one sure remedy for the concern that anything might go is the establishment of a principle that nothing goes. But the need for predictability cannot justify that solution. A constitutional amendment that established extremely high and progressive rates for income and estate taxes would provide as much certainty as one that repealed them. In fact, taxes and transfers have been treated as standard kinds of legislation, enactable by simple majorities of both houses of Congress and subject to veto by the President. Yet, those laws have been subject to remarkable continuity rather than to erratic fluctuation. Major structural changes in the tax base or the scope of transfer programs have at times been phased in gradually, often with a grandfather clause. Unlike some other nations, we have not imposed federal taxes on the holding of wealth (as distinguished from property income or the transfer of wealth), in part because the initiation of such a tax might be "retroactive." The political process has displayed a great respect for continuity; on the whole, I find that reassuring.

The much graver danger is that the democratic process may become myopic in confronting the tradeoff between equality and efficiency. Much of the gain from a redistributive program is immediate, while many of the efficiency costs are delayed and, indeed, less obvious than the gain. When the lowest 51 percent of families in the distribution have only a quarter of all income and only one-twentieth of all wealth, is there an adequate safeguard against a demogogue who might irresponsibly promise a majority of voters a "fair share" of the pie?

Some market enthusiasts have a recurrent nightmare in which the mob wrecks the bakeries in its quest for bread. As I see it, that nightmare has not materialized in American political and economic life, but I suspect that the security of the wealthy has been ensured because money has bought political power. Indeed, I believe that the use of money to acquire voting rights has blunted the political expression of majoritarian preferences for equality. As a result of recent legislation to curb the counterfeiting of votes, we will get a test of the operation of a more democratic political process.

At the moment, we are experiencing a disturbing divisiveness of attitudes. Recent efforts to curb the market's transgression on equal political rights have frightened those who hold the bulk of the wealth (and think that they therefore hold the bulk of the truth), and have aroused antidemocratic political sentiments. There is a more obvious growth of anticapitalistic sentiments by the nonaffluent. Profits and rich are often dirty words in the halls of Congress. The rationing and allocative functions of the price system are blithely ignored by many of our legislators. Instead of blending the values of capitalism and democracy, many are pitting them against each other. Instead of compromising, we are polarizing. The nation sorely needs a serious dialogue and a major educational undertaking to develop the enlightened attitudes of compromise, and I hope that this conference will help meet that urgent national need.

INDEX

Ackley, Gardner, 103
Acquired assets, contribution and,
41–42
Advertising, 57
Aids-in-kind, 109–10
Aid to families with dependent children
(AFDC), 108
Allegiance, self-interest and, 47–48
Anticompetitive laws, 28n30
Attitudes: on government, xi; on market, 140–43
Attitudinal impacts of taxation, 97–98

Banfield, Edward C., 78
Bans on exchange. *See* Exchange of
rights, bans on
Bernstein, Carl, 38
Bill of Rights, 5
Biological differences, 42–43
Bonuses, income and, 70
Borrowing money. *See* Capital, unequal
access to; Debt
Bribes, 24
Buchanan, James M., 11–12n14
Bureaucracy. *See* Government
Burke, Edmund, 7
Business expenses, 95

Campaign financing, xii, 23–24
Capital, unequal access to, 77–80, 97,
132

Capital-gains taxation, 101, 101n20,
112
Capitalism: alternatives to, 50–59,
61–62; democracy and: *See* Democracy, capitalist; efficiency and,
48–50, 62; freedom and, 32, 34–39,
53n25, 54n28; income and, 32, 62,
137; institutional structure of, 4–5;
laissez-faire, 12n15, 138; market
rewards and, 39–48; market society
and, 12n15; public support for,
31–33; survival, right to, 17
Carlin, Jerome E., 22n27
Charity, 17, 17n20
Checks and balances on market, 13
Chief executive officers, compensation, ix
Child labor, 19
China-U.S. trade, ix
Civil rights. *See* Rights
Clinton administration, viii, viiin3
Codes of conduct, 25, 26–27
Coercion by state, 34, 138–39, 139n29,
144–46
Collective ownership, 34–39. *See also*
Socialism
Collectivized economies, 37–38, 50–59,
54n28. *See also* Socialism
Communist Manifesto, 98
Comparative advantage, rights and, 7,
15, 122

ARTHUR M. OKUN

Arthur Melvin Okun is widely considered among the most important macroeconomists of the twentieth century. Born in 1928, in Jersey City, New Jersey, he received his A.B. and his Ph.D. from Columbia University and went on to teach economics at Yale University. In the 1960s he served as a senior economist, member, and, finally, as chairman of the Council of Economic Advisers in the Kennedy and Johnson administrations.

When Okun left the CEA, he joined the Brookings Institution. In 1970, he cofounded, with George Perry, the *Brookings Papers on Economic Activity* (BPEA), which is still among the world's most prestigious economic journals and currently boasts sixteen Nobel Prize winners among its authors and discussants.

Known for his wit as well as his compassion, Okun reacted to surging inflation in the 1970s by developing an economic indicator he dubbed the *Misery Index,* which charted the well-being of Americans by combining the unemployment rate and inflation rate. In the years since, Okun's idea of indexing misery has been both repurposed and refined to track happiness and well-being across all sorts of indicators.

When Okun died unexpectedly at the age of just 51 in March 1980, he was hailed as an innovative and effective policy economist who was unique in holding the respect and admiration of both academic economists and practical politicians.

Okun is today remembered as an effective mediator between the realms of economic theory and analysis and the development and implementation of public policy. In this realm, *Equality and Efficiency: The Big Tradeoff,* with its difficult questions about the uneasy relationship between capitalism and democracy, is most certainly Okun's masterwork.

Printed in the USA
CPSIA information can be obtained
at www.ICGtesting.com
LVHW101735090823
754735LV00004B/400